C000259815

HAUNTED

DOVER

HAUNTED
DOVER

LORRAINE SENCICLE

First published 2009

The History Press
The Mill, Brimscombe Port
Stroud, Gloucestershire, GL5 2QG
www.thehistorypress.co.uk

© Lorraine Sencicle, 2009

The right of Lorraine Sencicle to be identified as the Author
of this work has been asserted in accordance with the
Copyrights, Designs and Patents Act 1988.

All rights reserved. No part of this book may be reprinted
or reproduced or utilised in any form or by any electronic,
mechanical or other means, now known or hereafter invented,
including photocopying and recording, or in any information
storage or retrieval system, without the permission in writing
from the Publishers.
British Library Cataloguing in Publication Data.
A catalogue record for this book is available from the British Library.

ISBN 978 0 7534 4859 6

Typesetting and origination by The History Press
Printed in Great Britain

CONTENTS

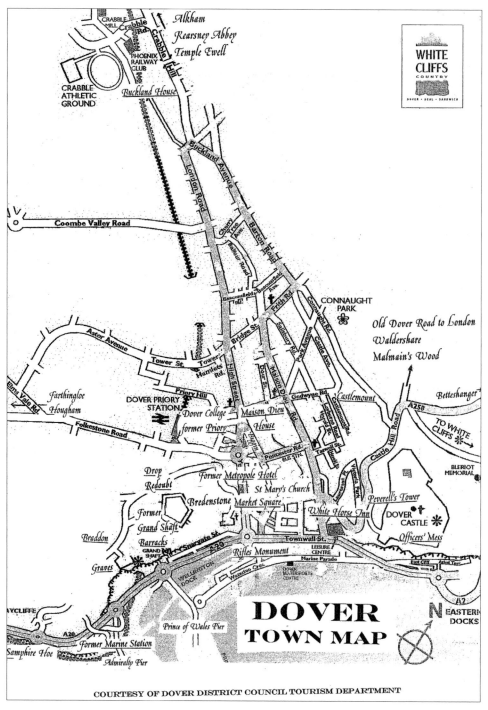

Map of Dover showing ghostly haunts. Basic map. (Courtesy of the Tourism Department, Dover District Council)

Introduction

Dover's documented history stretches back to prehistoric times and has left many ghosts and legends. The town and the immediate environs ghosts are not only of interest to the students of the paranormal, they are reminders of the people who once lived here and of the important place the town and harbour has played in history. Being such an ancient town there are no shortages of ghosts, so the ones I have chosen are those with stories to tell.

My thanks go to Graham Tutthill of the *Dover Mercury*, who encouraged me to first write these stories down. Also Graham Smith, the editor of the same paper, who published edited versions of many of them. To Jon Iverson and Bryan Williams of Dover Museum, along with Hilary Brenton, Liz Fairweather and Leslie Hanagan of Dover Library; Venessa Jupp and Keith Southey of Dover Harbour Board and Alan, my husband, for providing the photographs. To Lynn Candace, my eldest daughter, for her drawings. Also to Joanne Gray, Roy Porter and Rowena Willard-Wright of English Heritage (Dover Castle); Henry Kaczmarek of Dover Visitor Information Centre and Volunteers from the White Cliffs Countryside Project.

Lorraine Sencicle
July 2009

Ghostly Experiences

Kearsney Abbey

As a very young child I lived with my grandparents. My grandfather was a coal miner and their home was a colliery house in a colliery village. Like all such villages it was a close-knit community and my grandmother was recognised by all as having the 'gift'. Villagers, particularly in times of personal problems, would call on her but I was too young to understand what help she gave them. However, I still vividly remember one occasion when two distraught women came. A young man, brother of one and fiancé of the other, had been missing for a couple of days. Like most other colliers he was fond of 'beer, 'baccy and dogs' and was always short of money. Yet, like everyone else, come Sunday he would clean up and attend chapel. In fact it was after chapel the previous Sunday that he had kissed his sweetheart and said he was going for a walk alone. This did not concern her, as she guessed that the walk would be to join his mates in one of the local pubs. However, he never arrived and had not been seen since.

After telling my grandmother their concerns the women left. Although the evening was drawing in, it was still not dark enough to close the curtains, but my gran did. In the darkened room, lit only by the red embers of the fire, she sat in deep thought. I sat quietly beside her. After a while gran got up and opened the door of the large cupboard by the fire range. I had slept in the cupboard when I had been ill but it was normally used for storing linen. She gently patted the linen and started to speak, not to me, but to someone in the cupboard … but there was no one there. I was perplexed; what was happening? She ignored my questions and carried on having a conversation with someone I could neither see nor hear. She then turned to me and asked for paper and pen, which I brought to her.

Gran started writing and asking, whomever she was talking to, if what she was writing down was correct. When she finished she closed the cupboard door and lit the gas mantle. Gran then added more words to what she had already written. She put the paper in an envelope and bid me take it to the 'Bobby', who lived about three streets away. The village policeman was in, read gran's note, gave me a couple of sweets and told me to tell her that he would investigate. It was the next morning when the policeman called. They had found the body of the missing man, exactly where gran had said. The young man had committed suicide, possibly because he was in debt, his girlfriend was pregnant and he was about to be laid off.

As an adult I would recount the story and others in my family would also speak of gran's remarkable gift. She lived to be ninety and her friends from 'the beyond' came to see her right up to the end. However, I always remained sceptical. That is until I was researching my first book, *Banking on Dover*. Originally the book started as the framework on which to build the 1994 Dover Pageant. The Pageant Master, Mike McFarnell, had noted that the year was also the anniversary of the founding of the Bank of England and suggested that it might be an idea to use that as a theme. This was not without foundation, for it was generally held that High Street banking, as we know it today, started in Dover. My job, as Pageant Mistress, was to investigate.

Local records showed that an Isaac Minet, a Huguenot refugee, had founded a bank in Dover during the Wars of the Austrian Succession in 1744–1748. This was to help French

Dover Castle from the beach, 1803. (By Lynn Candace Sencicle, adapted from a painting by J. T. Serres)

prisoners, held in Dover Castle, to get money for their keep from home. Isaac's nephew, Peter Fector, was put in charge of this side of the family business and quickly built it up such that banking became the mainstay of the family fortune. Peter's son, John Minet Fector, was in charge by the time of the Napoleonic Wars. John was notably charming, popular and equally as astute in business as his father was. Following the Battle of Waterloo in 1815, the country went into a deep economic depression and starvation was rife. In order to combat this, John built Kearnsey Abbey, outside Dover, which provided badly needed employment.

When John died suddenly in 1821, the whole town turned out to mourn him, and after it was said that his ghost haunted Kearsney Abbey. John's son, also called John Minet Fector, took over the bank when he came of age. He was elected an MP for Maidstone, and eventually amalgamated the Fector Bank with the National Provincial Bank. Changing his surname to Laurie, his mother's maiden name, John junior, became the Chairman, a post he held until his death. By that time the NatWest, as we know it today, was one of the major high street banks in the country.

While researching the above, one question kept bugging me, where did the Fector wealth originate? To try and answer this, I spent several days researching the bank's early records that were, and still are, kept at the Centre for Kentish Studies at Maidstone. I found interesting facts, but nothing really enlightening and was about to give up when I came across a poster on forgery. Up until 1832 banknote forgery was a capital offence, so it would be a good illustration for the article. I asked the librarian for a photocopy – old records could only be copied on special machines. The young woman came back and apologised, for no apparent reasons both machines had stopped working and she had called the maintenance man. Was I prepared to wait?

I had packed my things up with the intention of catching the next train home, but the poster was good, so I agreed to wait. As it would be another hour before the next train I asked for another box of papers appertaining to the bank. This was brought me and as soon as I opened it the machines suddenly sprung into life! However, as I had missed my train I

Kearsney Abbey, built by John Minet Fector, 1840. (By Lynn Candace Sencicle, adapted from a drawing)

Dover Bank.

Whereas a well-executed Forgery

of the **DOVER BANK NOTES**, of *Ten Pounds*, with apparent Water Mark and Stamp Office Stamp, has just been discovered by us, we think it proper to give the Public the earliest Information of the said Forgery of *Ten Pound Notes*, to guard them against Imposition; recommending that, 'till the offending Parties are detected, for the speedy Discovery of whom no Measures will be spared, all Persons taking *Ten Pound Notes* will minute on the Back of them the Day taken, and the Name of the Persons they are taken from.

Dover, 9th March, 1819.

J. Minet Fector & Co.

G. Ledger, Printer, Dover.

Bank note forgery notice of 1819 issued by the Fector Bank. Up until 1832, bank note forgery was a capital offence. (Courtesy of the Centre for Kentish Studies)

started to go through the hundreds of transaction papers. Within seconds I came across what was a treasure-trove of archival material. It also went a good way to answer my question … John Minet Fector, and possibly his father Peter before him, had been East Kent's 'Godfather', running a massive smuggling racket! With this and other pointers I began to pull together the full story of how the Fectors made their fortune and why the local people particularly loved John senior. He had provided full employment by organised smuggling and to ensure that he knew what the Revenue Officers were doing, he had even built a new customhouse for them – right next to his bank! This led to another question; where exactly in East Kent did he run his illicit enterprise from, where did he hide the booty? It was not from his bank next to the harbour in Strond Street, Dover, nor from his town house in St James Street. The only clues I had was that caves were used with a passage to the sea, and that on the roof of the house in question, there was an observatory where John could watch for Revenue Cutters in the Channel. Both the bank and the town house were not sufficiently close to the cliff caves and the water table made a tunnel impossible. I knew that the bank possessed a significant number of mansions around East Kent. These had been acquired from defaulting creditors who had over-borrowed. I had looked at every one of them that still stood, and most did. Yet none were near any cliffs in which there were caves. As the pageant was drawing near, I decided to draw a line under that piece of investigation.

My husband was at work the night John Minet Fector senior called. I was asleep, when I suddenly woke up to see the tall, handsome figure, dressed in Regency clothes, standing at the foot of my bed! Strangely, I didn't feel frightened. He smiled and said just one word, the name of a house that I had looked at and dismissed a couple of weeks before. Although, I guessed, the Downs part of the Channel could be seen from the attic, it was built on a plateau and about half a mile inland, so there weren't any cliff caves. Next day, I went to investigate and on the way tried desperately to think how I should introduce myself – one can hardly say, 'John Minet Fector, who has been dead for 170 years, told me to call!' How I got through my introduction I cannot remember, but the owner, who asked for the name of the house to be kept secret, was interested. Certainly the house had caves, he said, brick ones, under the house and gardens for storing wine. However, he added, they must have been heavy drinkers for there are a lot of them! He went on to say there was even a tunnel that led from them, which he believed once went down to the seashore, but was now blocked. As we climbed to the top of the house the owner told me that he thought that it had once been an observatory of sorts and asked if John Minet Fector was interested in astronomy. When I saw the observatory, I told the owner its real purpose and could show him, without him telling me, a secret hiding place that could hold a man! My nocturnal visitor had helped me again! Do I believe in ghosts, what do you think?

The Old Lady and Her Dog in Peverell's Tower

Dover Castle
Dover Castle is reputed to be the most ghost-infested fortress in the UK! Visitors to the wartime tunnels have spoken of doors being banged by unseen hands and also of footsteps coming from behind. They have commented to guides on the realism of the lady re-enactor in Second World War uniform, who works in the Operations Room – when there

Dover Castle, 1786. (Courtesy of Dover Library)

were no re-enactors on the premises! Both staff and visitors have reported the sound of furniture being dragged across rooms and have also a seen a seventeenth-century cavalier arrogantly walking across the Castle Green. All of this has led to numerous investigations, as well as television programmes, on the paranormal activity at Dover's Castle.

The Castle's oldest, and arguably most famous, ghosts are the old woman and her black dog that haunt Peverell's Tower. The story was first written down by Genoise, a monk of Faversham Abbey. It begins at the time William I's forces razed the town to the ground, shortly after the Battle of Hastings. The King angrily ordered the town to be rebuilt and according to the story, William de Peverell was given the task of building the castle's first bastion, which bares his name. Genoise goes on to say that the building was dogged by problems from the start. Peverell, a hard taskmaster, was constantly putting his workers in danger, resulting in a number of serious injuries and fatalities. These Peverell blamed on his English workmen and brought in craftsmen from Normandy. Needless to say, this caused a great deal of resentment which came to a head when, without warning, tons of masonry collapsed, killing one of the new Normandy craftsmen. Although the accident was due to the lack of scaffolding, Peverell refused to accept that it was his methods that were at fault. For once both the English and the French workers were in agreement, but recognising that Peverell would not alter his methods, said that the tower was cursed. At this point they laid down their tools and went on strike – said to be the first strike in English history!

Peverell's first reaction was to throw the workmen into the town's dungeons and bring in a new set of workers. However, his most senior and best Norman craftsman, Geoffrey, suggested that a sacrifice may rectify the problem and would also be cheaper! At that moment an old woman with a black dog, whom daily sold victuals to the workmen, arrived. Seeing the pair Peverell shouted, 'Take ye that dog,' and he ordered that it should be bricked alive within the framework of the tower. Genoise continues, 'The ancient woman cried out sore that the dog should not die, nor be mured in any wise; and she resisted with what strength she had.' To which Peverell retorted, 'Thou cursed hag, give

Peverell's Tower, Dover Castle. (Courtesy of Dover Museum)

me thy dog, else will I mure thee also with the dog!' The old woman refused to let go of her dog, so Peverell ordered them both to be bricked in the tower. As the workman carried his orders, the woman screamed and the dog howled, so Peverell ordered a fanfare of trumpets to drown out their protestations. It was said that the woman ceased screaming after about a day but the dog continued to howl for several weeks and it was believed that it ate its mistress. After they were both quiet the construction went well and the tower with its archway, that we see today, was finished. Not long after the tower was completed, Geoffrey fell from the castle walls and broke his neck, while, according to Genoise, William de Peverell '…was cursed and buried neither in church nor hallowed ground, and none wist what became of him.'

Down the ages there have been numerous sightings of both the old lady and her dog in the vicinity of Peverell's Tower, and even more people have reported hearing a dog howling from inside the walls. The Abbey of Faversham, to which Genoise is reputed to belong, was not founded until 1147, therefore the story was either second hand, or alternatively set in a later era than given credit. The latter is likely to be correct, for although William I's forces did burn the town and he did order a new castle to be built, this was in the valley. The Castle on Eastern Heights was started in the days of Henry II (1154–1189). Most of the building took place between 1181 and 1188. It is recorded in the Pipe Rolls that the nation contributed £4,900 to the total cost of £7,000. Henry designated eight Barons to provide knight's service and each provided men, or paid scutage (a form of tax), for a designated number of weeks and in return the Castle towers were named after them. One of these knights was Peverell, who provided fourteen men for twenty weeks. However, the eastern section of his tower, which includes the D-shaped section in which the old lady and her dog are said to be incarcerated, was not constructed until the reign of King John. This later addition was in order to join up with the internal wall defences and were finished in the reign of Henry III.

The Lady Who Stayed the Night at the Officers' Mess

Officers' Mess, Dover Castle

Of the numerous ghosts reputed to haunt Dover Castle, the Lady in Red who stayed the night at the Officers' Mess is, perhaps, the most intriguing. A lady wearing red has been known to haunt the Castle for a very long time and is frequently seen by both staff and visitors today. She is usually seen falling or floating, depending on the commentator, down from the brick vaulting in the east corner of the Great Hall of the Keep. Whether this is the same lady who stayed the night at the Officers' Mess, and is still seen peering out of the windows there, depends on the storyteller. The Officers' Mess at the castle is the magnificent stone building in front of the ancient fortress and overlooking the Channel. At a cost of £50,000, it was built between December 1856 and June 1858, to house officers that were returning from the Crimean War (1854–56). It was designed by the famous architect, Anthony Salvin, and housed forty-five officers, their male servants and had stabling for twelve horses. The first occupants were the Bedfordshire Militia under Colonel Gillpin.

In December 1897, the 15th Company of the Eastern Division Garrison Artillery had just taken over from the 20th Company with General Sir William Butler in command. His wife was the famous painter, Elizabeth Thompson, who later wrote in her autobiography

The Keep, Dover Castle, where the Lady in Red is frequently seen. (Courtesy of Dover Library)

that, 'the Castle was the very ideal, to me, of a residence. Here was History, picturesqueness, a wide view of the silver sea, and the line of French coast to free the mind of insularity.'

The officers of the 15th Company soon settled into their quarters and as it was coming up to Christmas they planned to enjoy a few celebration dinners. Ladies, at the time, were not allowed into the Mess, but the officers' ladies were not forsaken, for Lady Butler gave memorable dinners at her residence in the Constable's Tower. These were likened to the banquets held in medieval times. On the particular evening of our story, dinner was being enjoyed in the Officers' Mess and Queen Victoria was about to be toasted. Suddenly, a beautiful, fashionably dressed young woman entered the room looking very distressed. She approached General Sir William Butler, and with great urgency told him that there was fire in the smoking room. A subaltern went in check and found that the chimney was on fire. This was quickly dealt with while the General sat the lady down and ordered her a light drink. Although he tried to assure her that the fire was out, she was insistent that the whole building must be checked. The officers, at the instigation, went to their rooms and checked, while everyone else checked general rooms, offices, cupboards and every nook and cranny of the building. They all assured the General that the fire was properly out … even the attic had been checked. The General, with the full company present, reassured the young woman, and started to ask who she was. However, the young woman got up and walked towards the door, vanishing before she reached it! The servants went through the whole building looking for her, but they all returned and reported that she was no where to be found! Further, there were no footprints in the light snow outside any of the outer doors! For the remainder of the evening the officers talked of nothing else but the strange woman fashionably dressed in red.

The young woman was still the main subject of conversation the following morning, over breakfast, but soon the routines of the day became the priority as the officers started their duties. Later that morning the young woman suddenly appeared, wearing the same red dress. She approached one of the officers, looking anxious. She went to a second and a third and eventually came to an officer who was, at the time, instructing his men by the stables. Much to their delight she insisted that he leave what he was doing and return to his room immediately. At first he ignored her request, but the Lady in Red was so insistent that in the end, and with his men's encouragement, he agreed. By this time other officers had joined the group and to them the young woman, smiled, curtsied and walked towards the castle through the virgin snow. She then just vanished without leaving any footprints!

When the officer reached his room, which was high up in the Mess, he saw smoke coming from under the door. He immediately raised the alarm and the barracks fire brigade was quickly on the scene. As there was a serious danger that the adjacent artillery magazines would explode, flag signals were flown from the Castle to summon help from troops at the Western Heights. However, by the time they had arrived the roof of the Mess was well alight. Dover police were called, as in those days the town's police were also in charge of firefighting. They requisitioned horses to haul their fire engine up to the Castle and local men joined them to help fight the fire. Meanwhile the people of Dover congregated on the seafront and in the Market Square to watch. Finally the fire was put out but the damage was estimated to be in excess of £2,000. Investigations that followed suggested that the fire was caused by wood smouldering in the roof following the chimney fire of the night before. The officer, whom the Lady in Red had approached, was called to

Dover Castle Officers' Mess. (Courtesy of Dover Museum)

answer before General Butler. He denied any knowledge as to whom she was and swore that she had not spent the night with him. Other officers testified that they had not seen her from the evening before until she appeared in the yard outside the Officers' Mess the next morning. The servants, who attended the room where the officer slept, said that there was no evidence of a woman having stayed the night. In the end, on the evidence available, the officer was cleared and it was generally believed that the Lady in Red was the same one who haunts the Keep.

The Officers' Mess, or to use its correct name, Officers' New Barracks, continued to provide accommodation for the garrison into the 1950s. Plans still exist to show what changes and modifications took place after the great fire to meet the needs of twentieth-century officers. Following the closure of the Castle Barracks, the Immigration Service used the west wing of the building for some years. The eastern half of the Mess was radically altered in the 1970s in preparation for a new visitor centre. This was to include a restaurant, exhibition and retail space as well as space for audio-visual presentations. National economic problems stopped the plans progressing, leaving a massive open space from the ground floor to the roof, which is said to be visually impressive. Since then, additional alterations have been made to meet the conservation needs of the building and recent work has included the introduction of new flooring in the western block, masonry repairs to external elevations and overhauling of the roofs. However, the eastern block remains a great empty cavern but, according to Castle officials, the Lady in Red is often seen peering out of windows of would-be rooms, which no longer have floors!

Braddon – The Ghost Village That Became a Reality

Braddon, Western Heights

Western Heights, the bleak cliffs that overlook Dover from the west, have been the haunt of ghosts and the subject of myths for thousands of years. It is also here, and on the Eastern Heights, where the Ancient Britons congregated in 55 BC when Julius Caesar and his conquering expedition sailed into the River Dour estuary. These forces must have looked fierce, for Caesar and his troops sailed out on the next flood tide and landed at Walmer, to the east. In the summer of AD 43, Claudius Caesar ordered the Romans to invade again. This time they landed at Richborough, near present-day Sandwich, where they built a great fort. Nonetheless, a further visit appears to have convinced the Romans that Dover could also make a good maritime base. Excavations show that about AD 130 the Romans built a base for their fleet, or *Classis Britannica*, on the Dour estuary. This covered some two acres west of the present day Market Square, under the Western Heights. On the top of both Heights they built lighthouses, or *Pharos*, as they were called. The Pharos on the Eastern Heights still stands, but the one on Western Heights eventually fell into disrepair. The ruins, locally nicknamed 'the devil's drop of mortar', became synonymous with the ultimate act of punishment when felons were thrown over the cliff to their death from there. This added to the eerie reputation of the Heights with many older Dovorians telling tales of hearing the screams of the condemned on dark, moonless nights.

During the Middle Ages, hanging replaced hurling felons off the Heights and this took place near the junction of the present High Street, Bridge Street, London Road and Tower Hamlets. This was, for centuries, outside the town's walls and there is a Dover Society Plaque that marks where the gallows once stood. The adjacent Eagle Inn has

Bredenstone, Western Heights, 1842, with the castle in the background. (Courtesy of Dover Museum)

Foundations of the Knights Templar Church, Braddon. (Courtesy of Dover Museum)

a reputation of being haunted by someone who had wrongly been hanged there. Also in medieval times the Knights Templars built a small church on the Western Heights, the foundations of which can still be seen. The Templars had their main house outside Dover at Ewell, now called Temple Ewell. Around both properties villages developed, and the one on Western Heights was called Braddon. However, in 1312 the Knights Templars' had been outlawed and most of their properties transferred to the Knights Hospitallers. The old church on the Heights became the village church of Braddon, the ghost village at the centre of this story.

1347 saw the Black Death sweep across Europe, and England was at war with France. Edward III had just won the battle of Crécy the previous year, and shortly after his troops triumphantly marched into Calais. The town had been held under siege for eleven months and the people of Calais were starved into submission. In an attempt to save the population from atrocities at the hands of the English troops, six Calais Burghers offered themselves to Edward as hostages. The King was about to have them executed and allow his troops to do their worst when Phillippa, his wife, pleaded with him. She asked for the Burghers and their servants to be sent to England as hostages, and to make Calais an English possession. The Burghers, so the story goes, landed at Dover and were to be taken to the Knights Hospitallers main house at Temple Ewell before journeying to London. Their entourage was housed at Braddon but within hours of their arrival in the village, one of the servants fell sick and died. Soon, the remaining servants and inhabitants of Braddon started to develop large painful white lumps in the armpit, followed by a rash, coughing, chest pains, fever and vomiting of blood before dying. The servant had brought the Black Death to England. Recognising the disease and how contagious it was, the Knights Hospitallers sealed Western Heights and refused to allow anyone to leave the area. Eventually all the inhabitants of Braddon and the French servants were dead. The disease, however, had been contained. The town, in honour of the people of Braddon, decided to hold a celebration the following summer, near the old Pharos. This they renamed Bredenstone for the bravery of the people of Braddon.

Unfortunately by the following summer the plague had found another in-road into England, but this time it was not contained. By the summer of 1349, nearly one million people in the country had died. As for the celebration for the heroic villagers of Braddon, that was forgotten. For the next few centuries Western Heights was used for cow pastures but the area around the Bredenstone was kept at a wary distance, in case the people of Braddon returned to reap vengeance. In 1666 the plague again visited Dover and between 400-500 of its victims were buried near to where Braddon once stood. This area was called 'Graves,' and still has a reputation for being haunted by zombie-like creatures swathed in dirty white shrouds. In 1660, Charles II landed at Dover, heralding the Restoration of the monarchy. Eight years later, as a token of gratitude to the people of Dover, Charles II nominated his brother, James, Duke of York, Lord Warden of the Cinque Ports. The installation took place, for the first time, on the Western Heights near the Bredenstone. It takes very little imagination to appreciate the crowds, the salutations, and fanfares that attended this great event. Indeed, the noise was so loud, it was said, that it would 'wake the dead' and according to legend, that is exactly what happened, for the ghosts of the ancient villagers of Braddon had joined the throng! Within a year James had upset his brother so a new Lord Warden was installed and again the Bredenstone site was used. This time closer vigil was kept on those who attended and again villagers, 'dressed in clothes of yor', came from the lost village of Braddon! In fact, the ghost villagers of Braddon attended every Lord Warden installation on Western Heights up until 1891, when the last installation of a Lord Warden took place there. It was generally believed that the ghosts of Braddon

Installation of Lord Duffering by the Bredenstone on Western Heights. (Courtesy of Dover Museum)

villagers attended in the belief that the ceremonies were being held for their benefit and that is why they have not been seen since 1891.

The story would have ended there with just a note saying that during the Napoleonic Wars the Western Heights were heavily fortified and these, with later additions, played a leading part in defences during subsequent hostilities. In 1954 part of the Western Heights fortifications, the Citadel, was taken over by the Home Office for use as a prison. Two years later the Prison Commissioners relinquished it to HM Borstal Institution, which eventually became a Young Offenders Institute. During that time, houses for officers were built on the area where once the village of Braddon had stood. In Calais, on the other hand, there is a magnificent sculpture by Auguste Rodin depicting the 'Six Burghers of Calais', who gave themselves as hostages to save the people. This stands in all its magnificent glory of front of the Town Hall there. As for the villagers of Braddon, their heroic deed and their ghostly attendance at Lord Warden installation ceremony would have become a myth. However, following the closure of the Young Offenders Institute, the officers' houses were sold, many bought by their occupants. Led by Richard Pimblett, the residents applied for and successfully gained village status for the estate, taking the name of Braddon at midnight on 20 October 2001. Thus the ghost village eventually received the recognition it deserved and it is hoped that in the future, celebrations will be again held on the Heights and perhaps the ancient villagers will be seen again.

Peter the Drummer Boy

Drop Redoubt, Western Heights

The Western Heights, besides being haunted by ancient Britons, felons who were thrown to their death, zombie-like creatures that were buried there during the great plague of 1666, and the heroic villagers of the ancient Braddon, also boasts of other ghosts. The most famous of these is Peter the Drummer Boy. Back in 1779 England was not only at war with her American colonies and France, but also Spain. As the combined fleets of France and Spain were greater than England's, Lord North, the Prime Minister, was concerned over the possibility of invasion. That summer saw a number of defensive measures being undertaken in Dover, including earthworks on the Western Heights. Then all went quiet until 1799 and the French Revolution. On 10 November that year, Napoleon Bonaparte seized power in France and the people of Dover braced themselves for repercussions. Plans were made for a major defensive programme in Dover, which included the Western Heights. Then, on 18 May 1804, Napoleon Bonaparte declared himself Emperor of France and the defensive programme was put into operation. Western Heights was turned into a major, new style fortification, the centre of which was the Drop Redoubt. Unlike the Keep at the Castle, which was built towering above the Eastern Heights, the Drop Redoubt is *within* the Western Heights. The word 'Drop' came from the local name for the remains of the ancient Pharos -'the devil's drop of mortar'. At the same time the Citadel, Military Hospital and the Grand Shaft Barracks, which provided accommodation for fifty-nine officers plus 1,300 NCO's and privates, were built.

As the barracks were above the town, the Grand Shaft, a unique 140ft high triple spiral staircase, was also built. This was designed to move troops very quickly from the Grand

Grand Shaft Barracks, 1850. The entrance to the Grand Shaft can be seen behind the couple on the right. (Courtesy of Dover Library)

Shaft Barracks and Drop Redoubt Fort down to the harbour to meet any invasion force. It was also used as a quick route for the soldiers to Snargate Street, in the Pier District, at that time the main commercial area of Dover and where most of the public houses and brothels were situated! The three staircases were respectively designated for 'Officers and their Ladies; Sergeants and their Wives; Soldiers and their Women'.

Peter Watson was a drummer boy stationed at the Western Heights garrison and his job was to tap out drum messages that ordered the comings and goings of the military. He also helped the Quartermaster by running errands and helped him to carry the garrison pay from Fector's bank, on Strond Street, adjacent to Custom House Quay at the harbour. To get to Strond Street the two soldiers used the quickest route, down the Grand Shaft triple staircase. The Quartermaster used the sergeant's staircase, Peter the one designated for privates. On the day that the story starts, on reaching Snargate Street, Peter waited for the slower, older and much fatter Quartermaster, who eventually arrived and they quickly crossed Snargate Street to Strond Street and entered Fector's bank. There the owner, John Minet Fector, handed over the money in large bags. The Quartermaster and Fector passed the time of day with the Quartermaster commenting on the amount of promissory notes (the forerunners of paper money), which he saw as worthless. These, the Quartermaster gave to Peter to carry, while he took the heavier and, to his mind more valuable, gold and silver coinage.

On the fateful day, as usual, at the bottom of the Grand Shaft the Quartermaster asked Peter to wait for him at the top, saying that as Peter had the lighter load, he would get to the top first. At the halfway point the Quartermaster rested and looked through the window that faced the centre of the shaft. Through it he could just see that Peter had almost reached the top. The Quartermaster continued to the top of the staircase and wiped his brow. He still had steep steps outside to climb before he reached barracks and shouted to Peter to wait. Eventually, the Quartermaster arrived at the top but could not see Peter anywhere. He called out for the youngster, but no one replied. Assuming that Peter had gone straight to his office, the Quartermaster went there, but it was locked, he had the key. Still Peter was no where to be seen and the Quartermaster raised the alarm. The day passed and Peter was not found and it was assumed that he had run off with the money, so the hue and cry was called but Peter was not found. When the duty bugler went to sound the Last Call that evening, from the walls of the Drop Redoubt, he thought he heard the

Grand Shaft Entrance in Snargate Street. (Courtesy of Dover Museum)

Drop Redoubt, where Peter the Drummer Boy haunts. (Courtesy of the White Cliffs Countryside Project)

distinctive rat-tat-tat of Peter's drum. This he reported and the duty sergeant ordered a full search but Peter was still not found. The following morning, the reveille bugler also reported that he too had heard the rat-tat-tat of Peter's drum, saying that it came from below the Drop Redoubt ramparts. Several soldiers went to investigate and saw what they thought to be Peter's legs sticking out from under a bush below. On further investigation they were shocked to find the headless corpse of Peter! In his hands were shreds of the bags that had previously held the payroll. Peter's murderer was never found but since that time the rat-tat-tat of Peter's drum has been, and still is, heard around the Drop Redoubt.

In the mid-1950s the part of the Western Heights fortifications that had housed the Drop Redoubt, the Grand Shaft Barracks and the Grand Shaft were handed over to Dover Corporation. They decided to use part of the Heights for industrial purposes; the four miles of moats as rubbish tips and the remainder for London overspill housing. Although in 1962 the Ministry of Public Building and Works scheduled part of the Heights as an Ancient Monument, the council dismissed this as a 'piece of nonsense', which led to a public outcry. After making a token start, the Corporation abandoned their scheme, which was then followed by years of neglect. Eventually, in 1985, the Grand Shaft triple staircase

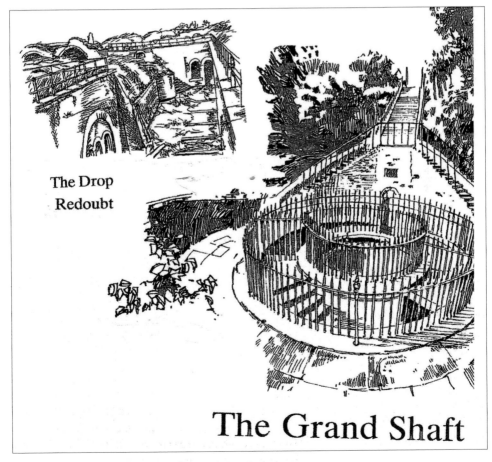

Grand Shaft and Drop Redoubt. (Courtesy of Dover District Council Tourism Department)

was restored and two years later, the Drop Redoubt opened to the public for the first time. In 1986, Dover District Council proposed that the site of the former Grand Shaft Barracks was to be allocated for housing and a hotel. Some 4,300 locals signed a petition opposing the idea and the author, with the help of her husband and fellow Dovorian, Jack Philips, took the proposal to a Local Plan inquiry with the outcome that the Planning Inspector supported the objector. The entire site was subsequently given Ancient Monument and Conservation area status and in 1995, an impressive replica entrance to the Grand Shaft staircase was built. Since then, cleaning up and preservation has relied on volunteers from the Western Heights Preservation Society and members of the White Cliffs Countryside Project (WCCP). The WCCP organise walks around the Western Heights and along with the many other ghosts, Peter's ghost has become a tourist attraction.

The Ghostly Guards Protecting the Rifles Monument

Rifles Monument, Camden Crescent

The Rifles Monument, not far from Dover's seafront, between Camden Crescent and Cambridge Terrace, near De Braderie Wharf, is the abode of the next ghosts. Usually four young officers, in full dress uniform of the 1850s, stand, heads bowed, holding the butts of their rifles. If they are approached, they assume an attacking position and can look very menacing. They have been known to frighten tourists returning to the nearby Churchill Hotel late at night! Their story goes back to August 1861 with the unveiling of the Rifles monument. This was erected by the officers of the 1st Battalion of the 60th Rifles to their comrades who fell in the Indian Mutiny of 1857–9. With great pomp it was unveiled but within days, for reasons unspecified at the time, the Rifles were transferred out of Dover. Immediately the Dover Corporation received a letter from 'someone on high' in London, who demanded that the obelisk be taken down forthwith, for diplomatic reasons.

At the time every city and town in the country seemed to be outdoing each other with the number and grandeur of the monuments that were erected within their boundaries. Dover was no exception and the Corporation had drawn up a list of the great and the good with Dover connections, of which there were many. In fact, there were too many to be able to purchase a monument for each one and when someone had suggested a shortlist, this had proved so contentious that the idea was dropped. Yet here was a beautiful monument, which had not been paid for by the Corporation, and they had received a letter, from central Government, demanding that it should be pulled down! The Corporation saw only one solution to this; they bought railings to surround and protect the monument! Further, in answer to their wishes, shortly after, guarding it were four ghostly officers!

The Rifles were formed in 1800 as the 'Experimental Corps of Riflemen' to specialise in skirmishes and reconnaissance. Its members were hand-picked from other regiments, given a green uniform and armed with Baker rifles. Within a few months they had established their reputation and were gazetted as The Rifle Corps. The Corps quickly earned battle honours in the Napoleonic Wars, including fighting alongside Nelson at the Battle of Copenhagen in 1801 and Wellington at Waterloo in 1815. In 1835 the Duke of Wellington's son, an officer in the Rifles, was quartered in Dover. The Rifles went on

Rifles Monument, where the ghostly guards are seen.
(Courtesy of Dover Library)

to serve in South Africa, 1846–47, the Crimea in 1854–56 and in 1857, upgraded to a Battalion, their experience was called upon to help put down the Indian Mutiny. The East India Company, set up in 1600, ruled India at the time. The Company was supported by a number of British regiments, backed by three local divisions that made up the Indian Army. The latter soldiers were predominantly high-caste Brahmins but were treated with contempt by their British colleagues.

The sequence of events that led to the mutiny are well-documented and concluded with the rumours spreading throughout the Bengal division of the Indian Army. These were either that the grease used for the cartridges was from cattle that were considered holy by Hindus; or from pigs, which the Muslims saw as unclean. Then on 29 March 1856 a Sepoy, Mangal Pandy, ran amok. He and the Indian officer who failed to stop him were hung and the reaction was mutiny. Atrocities were committed on both sides. Over 200 British women and children were butchered at Cawnpore (now Kanpur) and at about the same time captured mutineers were tied to the mouths of cannons and blown apart. The Rifle Battalion were sent from England, arriving at Cawnpore four months later. There they immediately took up arms and captured two long fourteen-pounder guns that they manually dragged three miles over rough terrain.

The Rifles then moved on to Delhi, occupied by 30,000 mutineers. In September 1857 it was recaptured. Following this, and overcoming odds of ten to one, the Rifles were involved in the relief of Lucknowe and Oude (as it is spelt on the monument or Oudh or Awadh, as in official documents). Lucknowe was recaptured on 16 March 1858 and the Rifles immediately went to the province Rohilcund, recapturing it by 23 May. Although final victory was declared on 19 June that year in Britain, Lord Channing for the East India Company had declared the mutiny over some eleven days before. The Rifles returned to England in March 1860 and were based at Dover, having earned four Victoria Crosses. However, by that time Parliament was beginning to question the wisdom of how India was being governed. The East India Company was abolished by Act of Parliament and the British Government took over the direct administration of India which was to last until 1949.

It was for this reason that the officers were told not to go ahead with the commissioning of the monument, but they did. On the day it was unveiled they were ordered not to attend, but every one of the officers and all of their men marched into Dover from their tents on Western Heights. Attended by the Mayor, John Birmingham, and all the local dignitaries, and with full military honours, the monument was unveiled. It bears the motto, *Celer et Audax*, and the place names, Oude, Delhi and Rohilcund. The inscription reads, 'In Memory of comrades who fell during the Indian Campaigns of 1857, 1858 and 1859 erected by the 1st Battalion 60th Royal Rifles, August 1861.' On 7 November 1958, after over 150 years, the

Western Heights Camp of 41st Regiment by William Burgess 1856, similar to that occupied by the Rifles, when they returned from India. (Courtesy of Dover Museum)

1st Battalion of the Rifle Brigade was designated as 3rd Green Jackets and in 1966 further redesignation led to the formation of the Royal Green Jackets, dropping the sub-title of the Rifle Brigade in June 1968. They were based in Dover on many occasions.

Although Dover is now best known as a port, during the eighteenth and particularly throughout the nineteenth century, the economy rested heavily on the military personnel based in the town. Indeed by the end of the nineteenth century, due to the Dover garrison, the town was one of the top ten most wealthy in the country! After the Second World War, the Dover garrison was slowly reduced. The barracks on Western Heights closed in the early 1950s, followed by the Castle Barracks in 1958. Old Park Barracks, near Whitfield, closed in 1991 followed by Connaught Barracks closing on Friday 10 March 2006. This last act finally brought to an end over 1,000 years of recorded military history in the town and was greeted with sadness by the town. Albeit, next to the Rifles Monument are four ghostly officers who are still defending part of that record.

The Headless Body of William de la Pole

Market Square

Moving inland from the seafront, passing though Bench Street and King Street is the Market Square. Nearby, in AD 696, Withred, King of Kent, had the St Martin-le-Grand monastery built. Immediately following the Norman invasion the town was razed to the ground, including the monastery, but William I ordered another to be built. The new St Martin's was, at the time, arguably the largest and finest monastery in England, embracing three separate churches within its walls.

Canons that were only beholden to the King and God ran it, which infuriated the Archbishops of Canterbury. In 1134, St Martin's was relegated to a parish church when Dover Priory, which was responsible to the Archbishop of Canterbury, was built. Following the downgrading of St Martin's to a parish church, locals started speaking of the ghosts of the canons. Then with the Reformation, in 1535, the church was closed after which the building fell into disrepair. The last free-standing wall was demolished in 1892, by which time reports that the site was haunted had gained momentum. The last remnants of St Martin's were demolished in 1955, but stones were incorporated into the front of the new National Provincial bank (now NatWest bank), started in 1953. On the floor of the bank is a tiled ground plan of St Martin's, similar to the one reproduced here, but these days a carpet covers it. Nonetheless, the Canons still make their presence felt in the bank and around their former domain.

The opposite side of Cannon Street (spelt with two 'n's and named after an old Dover family – see page 34), in the Market Square, is Lloyds Bank. This building has one ghost, a headless

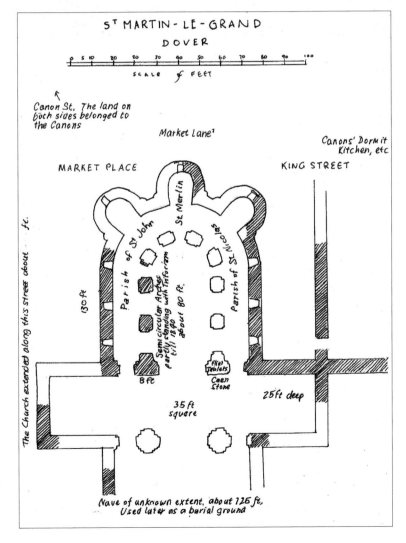

Ground plan of St Martin le Grand. (From Perambulation of Dover by John Bavington Jones, 1907)

The war-damaged National Provincial Bank during preparations for the Coronation in 1953. Nearby more Second World War damage can still be seen. (Courtesy of Dover Library)

man in medieval garb, but he has received lasting notoriety. William, as he is called, has been seen for centuries within that vicinity, usually walking towards the adjacent Church Street, where he disappears. In medieval times, on this site, stood St Peter's Church that superseded St Martin's in 1367 as the town's centre of civic life. St Peter's also housed the curfew bell, which was tolled to tell people to go home and lock their doors in the evening and rung to tell the townsfolk that it was time to open shutters and go out into the streets in the morning. The bell also doubled as an alarm when the town was under attack from the sea, something that happened frequently in those days. It was also in St Peter's that council meetings were held and where elections, both local and parliamentary, took place. That is, until 1581, when they were moved to St Mary's Church, following which St Peter's was demolished.

By that time, the headless ghost was believed to be William de la Pole who was born in 1396, the second son of the Earl of Suffolk. He had enjoyed a brilliant military career, appointed the co-commander of the English forces at the siege of Orléans, France, in 1429. At that time the King, Henry VI, was eight years old and had been on the throne for more than seven of them! The King's father was the illustrious Henry V, who had sailed from Dover to his victorious battle at Agincourt. With his triumphant troops, the King returned through Dover and was carried through the streets in great jubilation. Henry was to use the port on several occasions until his death in 1422, when his coffin was brought back through the port and carried through the town. The crowds that lined the streets were in deep mourning. Henry had recognised the strategic importance of Dover and thus had appointed his brother, Humphrey, the Duke of Gloucester, as Lord Warden of the Cinque Ports. In his will, the King also arranged for his son to be brought up by Duke Humphrey, thus making the Duke the most powerful man in England. Indeed, it was he who had appointed William de la Pole and was delighted with his victory at Orléans.

However, on 8 May 1429, Joan d'Arc triumphantly led a 4,000 strong French army into Orléans. The humiliated William de la Pole managed to escape but was later captured and held prisoner for three years until a ransom was paid. The victory at Orléans, together with the coronation of Charles VII, King of France, at Rheims, had a tremendous effect on French morale and a succession of French victories followed. Then on 24 May 1430, at the battle of Compiegne, Joan d'Arc was captured, handed back to the French and was subsequently burnt at the stake. The following December saw Henry VI of England crowned Henry II of France but by then French nobles, who had previously been allies of England, began to waiver. In the meantime, William de la Pole had returned to the English Court and was quickly learning the art of politics. July 1436 saw French forces besieging Calais, only twenty miles across the Channel from Dover. Duke Humphrey, as the Lord Warden, summoned the Cinque Ports fleet and attacked, forcing the French to withdraw. Nonetheless, French insurrections continued such that by 1439 a truce was mooted whereby Henry VI held onto lands in France but lost the title of King of France. This humiliated the King, who was now eighteen years old and thus found it hard to accept. He also insisted that his mother, Catherine, who was Charles VII of France's elder sister, was the rightful ruler of France.

Catherine, however, had other ideas. She not only accepted that the prerogative of lineage was through the male heir, she had secretly married Owain ap Maredudd ap Twrdw, a Welsh squire. As for Duke Humphrey, the teenage king was finding him irritating and wanted him out of the way. In 1441 Duke Humphrey's wife, Eleanor of Cobham, was charged with witchcraft and treason. Found guilty, she was imprisoned for life in Peel Castle on the Isle of Man. The reaction of Dovorians, who were very fond of Duke Humphrey, was outrage and Henry VI threatened the town with serious penalties. The constant wars with France were not helping Duke Humphrey's cause either, as they were draining the royal coffers. Thus, the search for peace became a matter of urgency and William de la Pole, by now Lord Chamberlain, negotiated a marriage treaty between Henry VI and Margaret of Anjou. The couple married on 22 April 1445 and in November 1446, Henry VI, under Margaret's influence, pardoned the people of Dover.

Although Duke Humphrey's power was waning, in February 1447 he called Parliament together at Bury St Edmunds. On arrival he was arrested and charged with high treason. However, he died before he could be brought to trial. This made William de la Pole, next to the royal couple, the most powerful man in England. In 1448 de la Pole was made the first Duke of Suffolk but the troubles in France were far from over and the next three years saw the loss of nearly all of the English possessions. De la Pole was held responsible and on 28 January 1450, he was arrested and imprisoned in the Tower of London. Initially he was sentenced to death, but this was commuted to five years in exile on the continent. As his ship was crossing the Channel, on 2 May 1450, it was besieged and de la Pole was beheaded. His headless body, which was dumped on Dover beach, was taken to Wingfield, Suffolk and buried. In the years that followed, nobles sought to replace Henry VI with Richard, Duke of York, the next in line to the throne. This resulted in the Wars of the Roses and eventually to the accession of Henry VII and the Tudor dynasty. Of interest, Queen Catherine and Owain Twrdw founded the House of Tudor. As for de la Pole's head, this was never found although, tradition said that it was Dovorians who had beheaded him to revenge the death of Duke Humphrey. Afterwards, it was said, they buried the head in a chalk receptacle in St Peter's Church.

Following the demolition of St Peter's church a grand mansion was built on the site, which quickly earned the reputation of being haunted by a headless man – the ghost of de la

North side of Market Square, today showing Lloyds Bank and the Dickens Corner, where St Peter's Church once stood. (Photo by Alan Sencicle)

Pole's body looking for his head. The house was later converted into tiny shops but the ghost of William de la Pole stayed still, apparently looking for his head. Then, in 1810, part of the old building was demolished and during the excavations for new foundations, a chalk cask with a skull inside was found. This confirmed that it was indeed William de la Pole who was haunting the buildings! In 1905 much of the north side of Market Square was demolished to make way for the new Lloyds Bank that we see today. During the excavations for the bank vaults, the crypt of the old St Peter's Church were discovered, in which there was a collection of bones. These were initially interred in St Martin's Cemetery that was, at the time, on the opposite side of the Square. The ghost of the headless William de la Pole though, has stayed on the north side of the Square, still looking for his head.

The Ghosts of Agnes Jaoman and Her Neighbours

Market Square, Queen Street and York Street area

St Martin's cemetery, until 1969, was near the south side of Market Square and it has left a legacy of ghosts. One of these was the poet Charles Churchill who died in 1764 and was later re-buried in Charlton cemetery. Adjacent to St Martin's cemetery was Tavener's Garden, which was used by the General Baptists of Dover for their burials. Samuel Tavener, after whom it was called, held a Baptist meeting at the back of his grocer's shop in Market Lane in the middle of the seventeenth century. At that time, houses used for religious worship but not of the Church of England could be pulled down and the religious fittings destroyed. The religious leaders would also be incarcerated and Samuel was no exception, he spent many years in Dover Castle for his beliefs. However, he did manage to keep his business going until he died in 1696, aged seventy-five. He was buried in his garden, as were members of his family and flock when they died. In May 1879 Tavener's Garden was transferred to St Mary's Burial Board and incorporated into St Martin's churchyard.

At the latter end of the nineteenth century, Dover businessman Richard Dickeson, who was also the Mayor, bought part of the St Martin's cemetery, including Tavener's Garden. On the site he built a wholesale grocery warehouse that grew into a massive commercial empire when he won a contract to supply the British Army. Knighted in 1884, Sir Richard went on to open warehouses in London, Aldershot, Dublin, Plymouth, Pretoria and Gibraltar. So well thought of was Sir Richard that when he died, on 13 October 1900, his body was on public view in the Council Chamber. A funeral cortege of over fifty mourners' carriages accompanied the coffin to St James' Cemetery. By that time his premises in Market Lane had earned a reputation of being haunted by ghosts dressed in Puritan garb, and locals did not like working there. During the Second World War the Dickeson building was badly damaged but afterwards reopened and was renamed Day Dawn House. Warren & Reynolds, wholesale grocers, then occupied it. In the late 1960s the building was demolished in preparation for the York Street bypass. At about the same time those interred in St Martin's cemetery were moved out and the cemetery was flattened. Following the opening of the bypass, the site was of considerable archaeological interest until the late 1980s when the White Cliffs Experience was built. This opened in spring 1991 but due to mounting losses closed on 17 December 2000. By this time it too had earned the reputation of being haunted. Not long after the building was converted to become the Dover Discovery Centre, which houses the library and a theatre. Although

Tavener's Garden, where the members of the General Baptists were buried. (Courtesy of Dover Museum)

Day Dawn House, previously the Dickeson Emporium, far left building on Market Lane, late 1960s, said to be haunted by people dressed in Puritan garb. (Courtesy of Dover Museum)

officially there have not been any reports of the building being haunted, some that work there say otherwise!

Nearby, on the green near the junction of Queen Street and York Street, is one of Dover's most frequently seen ghosts, Agnes Jaoman. She is usually sat whittling and is known to distract drivers waiting for the traffic lights to change. The first record of Agnes was back in 1588 when Mary I was on the throne. Agnes, an attractive widow, owned the Black Horse Inn in Queen Street. That year she was accused and:

> Justly proved that on St Simon and St Judes Day, at night, being a Friday, did roast a leg of mutton for her guests to be eaten…and was sentence to be put in the stocks with a shoulder of mutton roasting before her on a spit and then committed to prison until the Queen had mercy.

Dover's Mayor at the time was Thomas Collye, who was a brewer and a sheep farmer. Indeed, it was he who had supplied Agnes with the said mutton. Further, it was his wife who had reported poor Agnes and as Mayor, it was Thomas who found Agnes guilty and sentenced her! At the time there was a great deal of bitterness between Dover's Catholics and Protestants and Thomas Collye's wife was an ardent Catholic. However, twenty days after Agnes was sentenced, Queen Mary died and Elizabeth I ascended the throne. Because of the terms of the sentence, Agnes was released but she was very angry and full of vengeance.

In Agnes' garden there grew a spindle tree from which she would whittle skewers for local butchers and sheep farmers, including Thomas Collye. Agnes had a reputation for producing fine, safe skewers for although the wood is perfectly safe, the rest of the plant, including the berries, are very poisonous. After her release, Agnes was cutting some branches to make

The Cause is Altered Inn, believed to have been Agnes Jaoman's inn. (Courtesy of Dover Museum)

some skewers when the bright pink fruit caught her eye and she carefully picked several of them. These she roasted, taking care that the fruit did not contaminate anything else. When sufficiently hard, Agnes carefully ground the cooked berries and stored them safely away.

Dover's ruling elite, from Saxon times up until the Municipal Corporation Act of 1835, were the Freemen. It was from this body all holders of public office, from the Mayor down, were drawn. Also, for centuries, Dover held one of the finest and most popular fairs in Kent. This was to celebrate Dover's patron saint, St Martin on 11 November, and lasted ten days. On the evening before St Martin's Day, a feast was held in the Court Hall for all the Freemen of the town, their wives and their families. The Freemen provided the food and the non-Freemen, their wives and families cooked the meal and served the dignitaries. After which, they settled themselves on the ground nearby to enjoy what was left. Thomas Collye, as Mayor, gave his best sheep for roasting, but as Agnes served his wife with some of the succulent meat, she carefully sprinkled it with roasted spindle fruit. That night Mrs Collye fell ill and after a few days of terrible agony, she died. On the evening of his wife's funeral, Thomas was invited, by Agnes, to join her at the Black Horse Inn for a drink and a bite to eat. Thomas apparently enjoyed both the meal and Agnes. Indeed, before his year as Mayor was over, Thomas and all the other Freemen, including those with strong Catholic and Protestant sympathies, were regulars at Agnes's inn.

In 1559 Queen Elizabeth, concerned that troubles were brewing between the Catholics and Protestants throughout England, sent an Inquisition to find out. Of Dover, they reported that:

> the said Mayor, Jurats and Commonality were all in perfect peace, amity and concord, thanks
> be given unto God, and hath openly promised so to continue by God's grace.

In celebration, so the story goes, Agnes changed the name of her pub to 'The Cause is Altered'! For centuries afterwards the ghost of Agnes ensured that good humour prevailed.

Up until 1972 there was a pub called Cause is Altered, in the vicinity of where Agnes now roams. It was built near to the Cowgate entrance to the town and it had a plaque built into its wall stating this. However, although it probably was Agnes' pub, it was not given the name The Cause is Altered until 1826, when a new landlord decided to sever the pub's links with the smuggling trade. The last drink was served there on 22 March 1969 as a demolition order had been granted to make way for the then proposed York Street bypass. Public opinion led by the New Dover Group (now the Dover Society) wanted to retain two outside walls, including the one with the Cowgate inscription. The Corporation, on the other hand, wanted a modern town built of concrete and glass and the walls were demolished. However, much to their annoyance, they were unable to get rid of Agnes!

The Christmas Caroller at the Metropole

Cannon Street
North of Market Square is Cannon Street, named after a family who once owned land there. Walking up from Market Square, on the right is St Mary's Church and opposite is the Metropole building. It is here where the next Dover ghost resides. Like another of Dover's ghosts we will meet in this book, she is known for her singing voice. The Metropole building once housed a large, posh hotel, of that name. At the time of writing, the ground floor and basement are occupied by the Eight Bells Pub and above are flats. It was once the site of an ancient Dover inn, the Royal Oak, which was reputed to be haunted. This was demolished as part of the road-widening scheme in 1893, which enabled trams to pass through the centre of town. The Metropole was part of this scheme and as such, designed to have a grand frontage, epitomising the fact that Dover was one of the top ten wealthiest towns in the country at the time. The cost, including furnishings, was £17,000 and the Metropole opened on 18 October 1896, providing luxurious accommodation aimed at visitors to the Castle and the Western Heights barracks. It was also expected that naval personnel would also use the hotel, as part of Dover harbour had just been taken over by the Admiralty. To add to this, in 1893 work started on the Prince of Wales Pier and it was hoped by Sir William Crundall, Mayor in 1882 and twelve times after, that this would lead to Dover becoming a major port for visiting cruise liners.

The town turned out on 1 January 1902, to see the Prince of Wales, later King George V, open the pier named after him. As Sir William had predicted, the pier was ideal for docking ocean-going cruise ships. In order to attract these ships he, with the Register of Dover Harbour Board, Woolaston Knocker (later also knighted), travelled to Germany to persuade the Hamburg-America Line to use the port. The first transatlantic liner, *Prinz Waldemar*, tied up in July 1903 and for this, Sir William received a telegram of congratulations from Kaiser Wilhelm. Over the next three years an increasing number of ocean liners berthed at Dover with the result that the hotel industry, including the Metropole, thrived. However, work was still being carried out on the adjacent Admiralty Harbour, restricting passage. This, in 1906, caused the *Deutschland* to collide with the Prince of Wales Pier. The liner was so badly damaged that the rest of its voyage to New York had to be cancelled. After

CANNON STREET, DOVER

Metropole Hotel, Cannon Street, c.1913, where Adele can sometimes be heard singing just before Christmas. (Courtesy of Dover Museum)

that the cruise liner traffic declined, which had an adverse effect on Dover's economy. At the same time the Dover garrison was run down and the Admiralty were having second thoughts about using the port as a base for the Fleet. All of this affected the hotel business such that in 1912 part of the ground floor of the Metropole was let out to H.W. Alston outfitters and William Hollis, grocer.

It was around 1910 that Florence Smith, then the housekeeper at the Metropole Hotel, first welcomed Adele. She told Florence that she had first stayed at the hotel when her father brought her to see the liner *Amerika* on 12 October 1905, at the time the largest ship in the world. Adele went on to say that she loved big ships and with her father, was lucky enough to sail on the *Deutschland* the following year, but she was forced to disembark following the accident. Adele and her father stayed at the Metropole on that occasion, and that was the reason she had come back to the hotel. In fact, Adele was to book into the Metropole regularly for two to three weeks over the next four years. Within a day or two of her arrival, Mr Johnson would join her but the couple always left together. Mr Johnson always paid the bill and tipped the staff well and it was generally agreed that they made a lovely couple, especially as they were very much in love. It was particularly Adele that caught the attention of the staff. Not only was she always happy, singing softly, 'with a voice of an angel', with her golden hair piled high, she was also very beautiful.

By the autumn of 1914, the long peace was coming to an end, the war clouds were gathering and the Metropole hotel trade had fallen to rock bottom. Florence, by now the manager, knew that the hotel's days were numbered and was already looking for a

Amerika, Harbur-America Line, 1905, the largest ship in the world at the time. (Courtesy of Dover Library)

new situation. Nonetheless, the Johnson's were not put off and had arrived, as usual, with Adele preceding Mr Johnson by two days. On this particular occasion, a few days after the couple arrived, an elderly lady accompanied by a younger woman came into the hotel and asked to see Mr Johnson. The couple was out at the time so Florence arranged for tea to be served to the two ladies in the hotel lobby. Later, Florence said that she did not think that the old Mrs Johnson had meant to have a confrontation with her son in the lobby but when she saw him and Adele coming in and obviously preoccupied with each other, the old lady flipped. Florence was summoned by one of the maids as the younger woman had fainted. While Florence was dealing with her, the older lady, forgetting all her decorum, was authoritatively reminding Mr Johnson, that he was betrothed to the now prone young woman. In her anger she called Adele a 'trollop'! What happened next is unrecorded other than that the mother, son and fiancée left the hotel and Adele stayed.

In the weeks that followed Adele and Florence became friends. The manager learnt that the young couple had fallen in love and although Adele had means, these were not sufficient to meet the Johnson family debts. The younger woman, to whom Mr Johnson was betrothed, was very nice, of sufficient means and was keen to marry him. Although Mr Johnson had committed himself to an engagement, he did not appear to have the courage to stand up to his mother, or to make a clean break with Adele and marry his mother's choice. During this time Adele also accompanied Florence to St Mary's Church, across the road from the Metropole, as Florence had persuaded her to join the choir. Adele's voice so impressed the choirmaster that he asked her to sing a solo at the town's Christmas festival. She agreed and on that day Adele wore a 'beautiful blue gown' and 'enraptured' the audience as well as the choir.

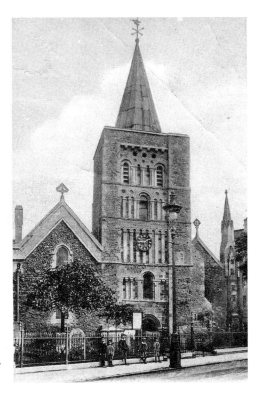

St Mary's Church c. 1900, where Adele and Florence sang in the choir. Courtesy of Dover Library.

In the New Year the hotel closed for good and Adele left Dover telling Florence that she would write. In March 1915 the Dover Motor Company, recently started by the Hollis family, made an application to take over the premises. In May, the contents of the hotel were sold and the rooms converted into flats. Florence found another situation but kept in touch with Adele, who wrote back saying that Mr Johnson had married his fiancée and joined the Royal Flying Corps. In another letter Adele said that she wanted to join the navy, but they didn't take women. She had written to her MP, who replied saying that the Admiralty were thinking of setting up a female 'arm' (The Women's Royal Naval Service or WRENS, was formed in 1917). Then Adele wrote to say that she had joined the Voluntary Aid Detachment, or VADs, as the volunteer nurses were called. The two women arranged to meet at Marine Station, before Adele embarked on her voyage across the Channel to the front line. Both women laughed when Adele commented that she was going on a cruise!

It was in one of the first floor flats, in what had been the Metropole Hotel, that the singer was heard. It was two days before Christmas 1916 and there was no doubt that the voice, singing Christmas carols, was beautiful. It could clearly be heard below on Cannon Street and people stopped to listen. However, when anyone went into the room where the singing came from, it stopped and there was no one there! Police Constable Booth investigated and reported the mystery to his boss, Dover's Chief Constable, David Fox. Chief Fox, perplexed, called on Florence and told her of the problem. The next day, Christmas Eve, Florence accompanied the Chief Constable to the flat and followed by onlookers, they entered the room. Immediately the singing stopped but in the centre of the room stood a beautiful young woman, with golden hair piled high. She was wearing a blue dress – it was Adele! Both women ran to each other and hugged, tears flowing from both their eyes. Then Adele just disappeared and the voice was heard no more that year. Chief Fox made enquiries and found that Adele had been killed in Belgium on 23 December. Her ghost had returned to Dover to say goodbye to her dearest friend.

The Metropole building, after the First World War, was to have a chequered history. 1929 saw the opening of the Plaza (later Essoldo) cinema in the rear of the building, while in the Second World War the basement was used as a shelter against bombing and shellfire. In 1968 the Essoldo gave way to the Rio Bingo Hall and in 1986, two years after the closure of Alstons, which had occupied the ground floor since 1912, plans were submitted to demolish the building. These were later withdrawn and Wetherspoon's took over part of the ground floor and basement for the Eight Bells. The flats above, which by 2004 had remained empty for fifteen years, were renovated at a cost of £1.5 million. During all of that time, around 23 December, there have been reports of a woman with a lovely voice singing carols from one of these flats, but nobody has actually seen the singer since 1916.

A True Relation of the Apparition of One Mrs Veal

St Mary's Church

Across the road from the Metropole building, in the vicinity of St Mary's Church, is the domain of Dover's next ghost. He is the son of one of the characters involved in a sensational eighteenth-century phenomenon that helped to launch the writing career of Daniel Defoe. George Elliot also used the story as the base for one of her characters in *Middlemarch*, and it starts with Mrs Veal. Although not married, she adopted the courtesy title given to genteel spinsters of the time. Mrs Veal was a pious woman who kept house for her only brother, William, a lowly customs clerk, in Dover. Their father had been a wastrel so as children the Veals had lived in increasing genteel poverty. Throughout that time, Mrs Veal's closest friend was Miss Lodowick, the daughter of Reverend John Lodowick, of St Mary's Church. Miss Lodowick married a prosperous Canterbury attorney and on becoming Mrs Bargrave, she moved to her husband's house in that town. From childhood, Mrs Veal had suffered 'fits', at the start of which she would talk very fast and on a subject totally unrelated to the conversation being held, then she would have a 'fit' and sleep for several hours afterwards. At the time of the story the two women had not seen each other for two years.

Although at midday on Saturday 8 September 1705 the weather was bright and sunny, Mrs Bargrave was at home sitting by an empty fire grate, nursing her baby daughter and feeling very miserable. Her marriage was a disaster as her husband was a cruel, philandering drunkard. She was also heavily pregnant with a second child, but she still had to do everything as her husband had sacked all the household help. Further, he had not returned home since he had left the previous morning and when he did, Mrs Bargrave knew that she would be physically punished for some misdemeanour that he would allege she had done. Mrs Bargrave was half watching next door's maid busy in the joining yard and started to think about her happy childhood days in Dover. Suddenly the doorbell rang and Mrs Bargrave, having put her daughter into the crib, answered it. On the doorstep, much to Mrs Bargrave's delight, stood her old friend Mrs Veal. She was wearing a smart new

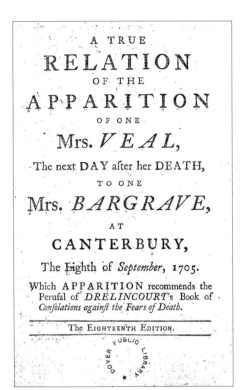

A TRUE

RELATION

OF THE

APPARITION

OF ONE

Mrs. *VEAL*,

The next DAY after her DEATH,

TO ONE

Mrs. *BARGRAVE*,

AT

CANTERBURY,

The Eighth of *September*, 1705.

Which APPARITION recommends the
Perufal of *DRELINCOURT's* Book of
Confolations againft the Fears of Death.

The EIGHTEENTH EDITION.

DOVER PUBLIC LIBRARY

*Frontispiece of the account of the apparition of Mrs Veal,
dated 1707. (Courtesy of Dover Museum)*

riding outfit, on which Mrs Bargrave commented as she showed her friend in. The next
door's maid, hearing the comment, looked through the open window and guessed that the
visitor was well to do. The two women quickly settled down to chat about old times and
common interests. So bright did Mrs Bargrave become that the maid outside commented
on this to her mistress later that day. However, about two hours after her arrival Mrs Veal
suddenly became agitated and changed the subject. This, Mrs Bargrave knew, was the sign
of an impending fit and tried to calm her friend down, but to no avail.

Mrs Veal was ranting only just coherently, saying that despite appearances she was not
very well off and that she was about to go on a long journey. The spinster went on to say
that she had given her brother the slip in order to see her old friend as she wanted Mrs
Bargrave to write to him on her behalf. Mrs Bargrave was mystified at this request, but
in order to placate her friend, she did as she was bid. Immediately Mrs Bargrave secured
pen and paper, Mrs Veal started to dictate, insisting that her friend wrote everything down
verbatim. The next door's maid later told her mistress that Mrs Bargrave was to tell the
brother, '…that there was a purse of gold in her cabinet from which she wanted him to
purchase a headstone for their parents grave.' When the letter was finished Mrs Bargrave
sealed and addressed it and asked the maid if she would take it to the Post Office. This, the
young woman agreed to do. Instead of having a fit and then falling asleep, as Mrs Bargrave
expected, Mrs Veal became quite calm. She told Mrs Bargrave that she would be taking the
stagecoach on the following Monday from her uncle's house, a Mr Walton, in Canterbury.
Mrs Bargrave agreed to meet her at his office and the two friends parted, Mrs Veal implying
that she was returning to Dover.

Mrs Bargrave spent the rest of the afternoon thinking about the strangeness of her friend's request but soon forgot about it when her husband returned home. He was drunk and, as expected, in a foul temper. The baby started to cry so he locked his wife and the child in the outhouse and then fell asleep. That night was particularly cold and the next morning, when he opened the door, Mrs Bargrave, who had used her own clothes to keep her baby warm, was visibly unwell. She attended to her infant daughter then went to bed for the rest of the day. The following day, Monday, Mrs Bargrave had recovered sufficiently to go to Mr Walton's office and meet her friend. When Mrs Veal did not arrive, the agitated Mrs Bargrave enquired of Mr Walton the whereabouts of his niece. The elderly gentleman took the young expectant mother to one side and told her the sad news that Mrs Veal had died. Shocked, Mrs Bargrave asked for details. Apparently, Mrs Veal had been taken ill the previous Wednesday 5 September and although the next day had recovered enough to go out, on returning home she fell into fits and died. The death took place on Friday 7 September – twenty-three hours before Mrs Veal had visited Mrs Bargrave!

What happened next was well-documented in all the broadsheets of the day. Suffice to say that Mrs Bargrave was known to be of good character and her description of what Mrs Veal was wearing was consistent with the outfit, worn for the first and only time by Mrs Veal, on the previous Thursday. However, William Veal, the brother, was adamant that Mrs Bargrave was a liar, saying that he had never received the letter even though the maid insisted that she took it to the Post Office and it was confirmed that it had been delivered to William Veal's address. He went on to say that Mr Bargrave's bad behaviour to his wife was well-known, and that her pregnancy plus being locked in the outhouse, '…had crazed her'. He could not, however, account for the maid's version of events other than saying that she was in collusion with Mrs Bargrave. Eventually William Veal allowed the cabinet, referred to in the letter written by Mrs Bargrave, to be opened in front of a number of witnesses. It was found to be empty which, he said, proved that the story was a figment of Mrs Bargrave's imagination. In the account, written shortly afterwards and held by Dover Library, the author finishes by saying,

> This Thing has very much affected me, and I am as well satisfied, as I am of the best-grounded Matter of Fact. And why should dispute Matter of Fact, because we cannot solve Things of which we can no certain demonstrative Notions, seems strange to me. Mrs Bargrave's Authority and Sincerity alone, would have been undoubted in any other Case.

St Mary's Church register shows that Mrs Veal was buried on 10 September 1705; no first name is given. On 15 December 1705, three months later, William Veal married Elizabeth Hughes, who was related to the Minet-Fector banking family. She was a wealthy, attractive widow from nearby Capel-le-Ferne and by the time of the wedding Mr Veal was no longer a poor customs clerk but a man of property. Not only that, but when the lucrative post of Controller of Customs became vacant, William Veal purchased it. He also became a well-respected dignitary within Dover until he died in 1729. The couple had eight children with the eldest, Young Veal, inheriting the family fortune. Young Veal became the Treasurer of Dover Harbour Board but due to his mismanagement, the Minet-Fector bank was forced to bail the Harbour Board out. This almost caused the bank to collapse, but it was not the end of Young Veal's ineptitude for he then fell 'on evil days'. His inherited estates were sold to pay his debts and he died in poverty in 1753. The general sentiment was

Dover Custom House about 1705, where William Veal worked. (Courtesy of Lynn Candace Sencicle)

St Mary's Church 1840, haunted by Young Veal. (Courtesy of Dover Library)

that, 'the sins of the father fell on the son'. Since then, Young Veal's ghost has haunted the vicinity of St Mary's Church, apparently looking for Mrs Bargrave to apologise.

The Ghosts of Archbishop Geoffrey and William Longchamp

Dover College, Saxon Street and Effingham Street
Dover Castle

This next story tells of two ghosts that reside in Dover. The first, Archbishop Geoffrey, haunts the area where once the Dover Priory, now Dover College, stood. The second is Archbishop Geoffrey's adversary, William Longchamp, who haunts Dover Castle. Their stories go back to the last days of Henry II in 1189. When Henry built the Dover Castle we see today, he saw his main threat coming from the country's Barons. Towards the end of his reign this changed when he faced a much greater threat from his legitimate and illegitimate children. His eldest legitimate son, Richard, (soon to be Richard I, the Lionheart), invaded Henry's French domains of Anjou, Maine and Tours. Of his illegitimate sons, Geoffrey Plantagenet was the only one who remained loyal to his father and Henry, in return, gave him the Archbishopric of York. Henry died on 6 July 1189 and Richard was crowned some two months later. On 1 December, Richard signed a new Charter for Dover, then within two weeks embarked on the Third Crusade from the port. His army consisted of 4,000 men-at-arms, 4,000 foot soldiers, and a fleet of 100 ships. Richard also took along with him the Archbishop of Canterbury, thus Geoffrey, as the designate Archbishop of York, became the highest ecclesiastical authority in England. In order to pay for the Crusade, Richard sold official posts to the highest bidder; the most senior civil post was Chancellor of England, who would also act as Regent while the King was away. William Longchamp, Bishop of Ely, paid £3,000 for this privilege and possibly due to Longchamp's appointment, Geoffrey went to Tours, France, to be consecrated as Archbishop of York. This took place on 18 August 1191. It should be noted that Geoffrey was not new to the ecclesiastical world, as a boy he had been entered into the church and also appointed Archdeacon of Lincoln. As an adult, Geoffrey found his true vocation in combat, indeed, his exploits were legendary and, at the time, far exceeded those of his half-brother, Richard. It was for these that Henry II had rewarded Geoffrey with increasingly higher ecclesiastical offices!

Richard had no love for Geoffrey so on hearing of his consecration sent strict orders that the new Archbishop was not to return to England until he, Richard, had returned from the Crusade. Failing his return, Geoffrey was not to be allowed into the country for at least three years after Richard's death. Within a month of his consecration, however, Geoffrey arrived at Dover to take up his new post. Kent historian, William Lombarde, vividly recounts what happened next. In essence, William Longchamp ordered Matthew de Clera, Sheriff of Kent and Constable of Dover Castle, 'to have a vigilant eie to his arrival, and that no soone as the Archbishop did set foote on land, he should strip him of all his ornaments and commit him to the safe custodie within the Castell'.

On landing at Dover, Geoffrey was asked to go with de Clera's men to the Castle but he refused. Instead, Geoffrey secured a horse and rode around the town to the Priory, at the far end of Dover. This took de Clere's men by surprise, for they expected Geoffrey to go

Dover Priory Gatehouse, early twentieth century. (By Lynn Candace Sencicle, adapted from a drawing by E. Piper)

to the church of St Martin-le-Grand, near present day Market Square, as it was the only place that could legally offer sanctuary. De Clera, was so sure that Geoffrey would do that, he had the church surrounded. Although the Priory, dedicated to St Martin of Newark and began in 1131, was Dover's motherhouse, St Martin-le-Grand Church had retained the right of sanctuary. At the Priory, even though Prior Osbern was unable to offer Geoffrey sanctuary, he did invite him in to lead prayers of thanksgiving 'to sacrifice to St Martin for his safe passage' and hear mass of his chaplains. Frustrated, de Clera's men blocked all the exits from the Priory in order to arrest Geoffrey when he attempted leave. Time passed and Geoffrey stayed within the walls of the Priory so William de Auberville, de Clera's second-in-command, forcibly entered. He demanded that Geoffrey take the oath of fealty to the King and Chancellor Longchamp and leave with him. Geoffrey responded by making it clear that he would take the oath to King Richard, but not to Longchamp.

The following day, Sunday, Geoffrey gave the Mass in the Priory Chapel, during which he excommunicated de Clera, Auberville and some of their men, thus effectively making them outcasts. De Clera, who attended the proceedings, marched out and angrily demanded that Geoffrey be kept prisoner in the Chapel until he capitulated. That evening de Clera, possibly realising that Geoffrey would not be in any hurry to leave the chapel, went to see the Archbishop and again demanded loyalty to Longchamp. Again Geoffrey refused and was escorted to a tiny cell within the Priory, where he remained prisoner for five days. On the sixth day Geoffrey demanded to be allowed to go to the chapel to pray. De Clera agreed but with the intention of arresting the Archbishop en-route. However, when Geoffrey emerged from his cell he was wearing his full Archbishop's regalia and in his hands he carried 'a cross ornamented with gold and ivory'. On seeing this, De Clera's men fell to their knees and begged forgiveness.

Interior of the Dover Priory Chapel, c.1850. (Courtesy of Dover Library)

Geoffrey entered the chapel, seated himself near the high altar and waited, as did Prior Osbern and the congregation of monks. De Clera, Auberville and the men whom Geoffrey had previously excommunicated entered the chapel, with cloaks over their weapons. Again De Clera demanded fealty and again Geoffrey refused. De Clera then asked Geoffrey to return to France, but this he also refused to do. Finally, throwing back their cloaks and revealing their swords, they knocked Geoffrey down and dragged him, feet first, from the chapel. Outside Geoffrey was offered a horse but he lay where he had been dropped. Eventually, the Archbishop's feet were tethered to the horse and he was dragged through the town and up to the Castle. Witnessed by both the monks and the townsfolk, it is written that they cried out, 'Ye cowards! Why do you drag him away in this manner? What harm has he done, he, an Archbishop, brother of a king and a son of a king?' Legend has it that Geoffrey was then taken to the castle where he was slain, but in reality this was not the case! That night, one of the worst south-westerly storms to hit Dover, which gave rise to the old Dovorian couplet, 'Blow Dover wind Blow, save Archbishop Geoffrey and kill his foe.' It is on such nights that the ghost of Archbishop Geoffrey is most likely to be seen. He is usually seen drifting between the Gatehouse and the Refectory of Dover College, as well as in the adjacent Saxon and Effingham Streets. It is also on such nights that the ghostly singing can be heard in the area where the chapel once stood.

Although Archbishop Geoffrey was dragged up to the castle, an expedition led by the Earl of Cromwell and a number of bishops saved him. At about the same time William Longchamp was arrested and Richard's brother, John, became the effective Regent of England. After a further seventeen tumultuous years Geoffrey died at Grandmont, near Rouen, France. On 16 November 1535 the Dover Priory was surrendered to the Crown and the land was given over to farming. The original Refectory can still be seen on Effingham Street. In 1871 Dover College opened and since then the College authorities have done much to restore what remains of the Priory. As for Longchamp, following his downfall he managed to escape dressed as woman selling cloth and wearing a green gown and a cape with long sleeves and a hood. He came to Dover, where he tried to

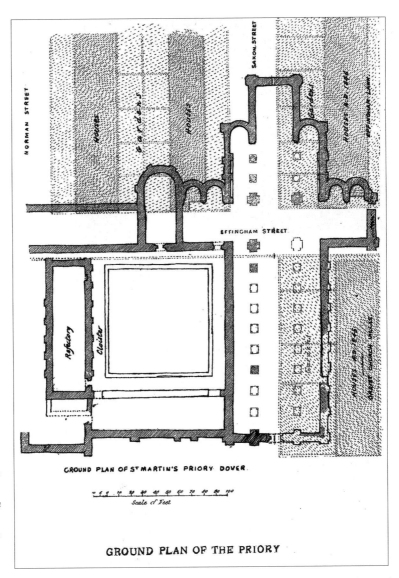

GROUND PLAN OF St MARTIN'S PRIORY DOVER.

Scale of Feet

GROUND PLAN OF THE PRIORY

Ground Plan of Dover Priory Chapel superimposed on a contemporary map of the town. (From Perambulation of Dover *by John Bavington Jones, 1907)*

board a ship for France. While waiting a local fisherman, thinking Longchamp was a woman, tried to take advantage of the disguised former Chancellor by putting his hand up Longchamp's dress! Realising Longchamp was a man, the fisherman cried out which brought some women to the scene. Although Longchamp's servant tried to drive them all away the women, seeing the cloth, tried to bargain for it. At this, Longchamp pretended that he did not understand them but the fisherman informed the ensemble crowd that Longchamp was a man and could speak English! At this the crowd dragged 'the monster by the sleeves and cape through the town, reviling, beating and spitting on him all the way, until they finally laid him by his heels in a dark cellar.' He was eventually released and on the 29 October was allowed to cross to the continent. Four years later he died, but his ghost returned to the town and still haunts Dover Castle!

The Ghost of Maison Dieu House or The True and Remarkable Story of Mary Gray

Maison Dieu House, Biggin Street

It is believed that most old buildings in Dover have a resident ghost and Maison Dieu House, in Biggin Street, is no exception. Built by the Royal Navy in 1665 to serve as the residence for the Agent Victualler, a recent paranormal investigation in 2007 has shown that it has a number of ghostly inhabitants. One of the most famous is that of Mary Gray. Although it was recognised that Maison Dieu House was haunted, the story surrounding Mary Gray was eclipsed for over a century by one of Richard Barham's Ingoldsby Legends characters, 'The Old Woman Clothed in Grey'. It was not until 2003, when Maison Dieu House was put up for sale, that Mary's story came to light and the building's ghost was correctly identified. Since then Mary has been given celebrity status as Dover town's most famous ghost!

Mary's story begins on 21 October 1688 when James II was on the throne. A letter had been sent to William of Orange in Holland, inviting him and his wife Mary, daughter of James II, to take the throne. In Maison Dieu House such monumental events were of little concern to the victualler's wife, Mistress Papillon. She was more concerned about her husband, Thomas, who was behaving very strangely. He had been coming and going at all hours of the day and night and on the previous evening had demanded that she and the children return to their country residence at Acrise. The fact that the 'season' had only just begun was not of concern to Thomas and the atrocious weather was not conducive to taking such an arduous journey. This she was confiding to Mary Gray, the children's nanny, with tears streaming down her face. To make matters worse, the evening before, Mistress Papillon said, she had seen her husband at the back garden door talking to a beautiful young woman. 'Her hood had blown off in the wind,' Mistress Papillon wailed.

Calming her mistress down, Mary suggested that she would hide behind one of the panels of the back garden room. From the vantage she could watch and if the young woman called again, she would be able to tell her Mistress what had taken place. Mistress Papillon was appeased, so calmly and coldly she ordered the other servants to pack hers' and the children's clothes as they were all returning to Acrise. That evening, Mary did as she promised and before long Thomas entered the room. He blew out his candle and opened the back door. The in-rush of wind caused the door to the closet, where Mary was hiding, to swing open and she feared that she would be seen. She gently closed the door to, but not before she caught a glimpse of Thomas's guest. Mary recognised the woman as coming from the Castle and she was indeed beautiful!

Expecting an amorous affair, Mary was much surprised to hear that the couple had other things on their minds. She listened carefully as the young woman told Thomas that although the weather was bad (a strong east wind was blowing), William of Orange had left Holland to take the throne of England and was expected in Dover the following evening. At the Castle reinforcements were expected to arrive by the next morning and that French troops were making their way across the Channel to back them up. Thomas contemplated what the young woman had told him. He replied that as William would be landing in Dover as arranged, he would still be brought to Maison Dieu House for the night before going on to London.

After the woman left Thomas did not leave the room, and some minutes went by then Mary heard a light tap on the back door. Thomas softly opened it and Mary recognised the voice of Robert Jacob, the elected Mayor of Dover. He had been deposed by order of James II's Privy Council and replaced by the detestable outsider, Edward Roberts. Thomas told Robert what the woman had said, to which the ex-Mayor replied that he too had heard that French troops had set sail to head off William of Orange or 'the Hollander' as both men called him. Robert went on to say that a group of men had met in the Market Square, only an hour before, and were getting ready to storm the Castle. However, Edward Roberts had them arrested and locked them up in the town gaol. After the ex-Mayor left, Thomas sat in contemplation for a few minutes then he too left the house, quietly closing the backdoor behind him. All of the evening's events Mary reported back to her mistress. When Thomas returned home later that that night, Mistress Papillon welcomed him with a warm hug and kisses and brightly told him that she and the children would leave for Acrise the following morning. Thomas didn't know what had caused the change of heart, though he was relieved, and promised that he would make it up to her.

The easterly wind was still blowing when Mistress Papillom and the younger children left in the first carriage the next morning for Acrise. Mary, with the older children, went in the second carriage, followed by a cart with servants huddled amongst the belongings. Thomas kissed his wife and children goodbye and rode besides the first carriage to the harbour. There the Mistress Papillon's carriage turned up the hill towards Shakespeare cliff and the Folkestone Road for Acrise. Mary's coach had not even reached the harbour when one of the children in her charge announced that he had forgotten something of vital importance and insisted that their carriage return to Maison Dieu House forthwith. Mary let herself into the now empty house and ran up to the attic where the nursery and missing possession was. As she picked up the article, she glanced out of the window, which overlooked the back garden of the house, there she saw the young woman of the night before. Mayor Roberts was manhandling her and her hands were tied behind her back. There were also soldiers from the Castle who were undertaking reconnoitre of the garden and the back of the house. Mary heard them try the locked backdoor and also the windows. She quietly returned to the carriage and told the driver that she was staying at Maison Dieu House, but he was to drive in haste to Acrise.

Returning to the attic, Mary could see both the back and front of the house without being observed. As the day progressed more of the Castle soldiers came and they hid behind the bushes. It was not until the evening, when it was growing dark, that Mary quietly crept down the stairs to her hiding place in the back room. It was sometime before she heard Thomas return to the house. She also recognised the voices of both Robert Jacob and Captain William Stokes. The latter had brought Charles II to England at the Restoration in 1660 and since had been elected the Mayor of Dover four times. Up until James II became King, he had been one of Dover's two Members of Parliament; the other was Thomas. Peeping out of her hiding place Mary saw, in the moonlight, that the soldiers outside had also heard the men's voices and they were collecting around the back door. She started to leave her hiding place and warn her master when the door to the room opened and Thomas and his companions entered. They were carrying candles. The back door suddenly burst open and the wind blew out the lights. Musket fire rang out and Mary fell, mortally wounded, onto her master. She had saved his life.

That evening about thirty Dover men successfully demanded the release of the men that Mayor Roberts had locked up and together with some 250 other locals marched up to

Is anybody there? Yes.
Spooky night with Mary

A team of paranormal investigators has attempted to find out if someone called Mary haunts Maison Dieu House.

Mercury reporter **Mary Graham** was one of those locked in the town council office overnight to see what would happen...

A GLASS shoots across the wooden table... a spirit wants to talk to us.

We are sitting in a filing room in the eaves of Maison Dieu House halfway through our paranormal investigation. Many years ago this could have been someone's bedroom.

Four of us have our index fingers lightly on the glass. Medium Brian Falker, from Thanet Ghostwatch, asks if there is a presence in the room. The glass slowly starts to move.

I'm not sure how it moves and will never be able to fully explain it.

We are not using a classic ouija board. There are no letters. But we ask the spirit to only move the glass if the answer to our questions is yes.

Mr Falker senses the spirit's name.

Are you Michael? The glass moves for yes. Were you a dignitary? Yes. Is your picture in this building? Yes. Do you like playing practical jokes? Yes.

We ask Michael if there is someone else who wants to speak to us. Yes.

The story of the ghost of Mary Gray, who reputedly haunts the town council, is well known. She worked for the Agent Victualler and his wife around 1688. The family was preparing to leave the house around the time

of the Glorious Revolution which saw the overthrow of James II by Parliamentarians and William of Orange. Mary wanted to stay behind and was shot.

Answering our questions, Mary tells us that she was killed at 18 and that she did try to warn of the trouble brewing.

Councillors and staff often say that they sense Mary's spirit when weird things happen in their office, such as paintings crashing down and the doorbell makes "Mary's chime," when it sounds for longer than the standard "ding dong".

So we ask Mary: Do you like playing jokes on the councillors? Yes. Do you particularly like playing jokes on Tracey Hubbard, the allotments officer? Yes. Is your surname Gray? No answer.

Belief

Are there other spirits in the building? Yes, five apparently.

Later, when I'm alone, I try and push the glass with my finger in the same place. All I do is knock it over.

"Sceptics would say that the glass moves because of very small involuntary pulses in your fingers and muscles," says Thanet Ghostwatch's Keith Campbell.

"The key to what we are doing rests on your belief."

The group also uses small

"trigger" objects, placed in talc, to see if they have moved during an investigation.

In one room the trail in the talc almost forms an MG. It could be Mary Gray. Perhaps wishful thinking. It might be Mary Graham. Spooky.

We sense more paranormal activity. There is a feeling of sadness coming from town clerk Mike Webb's office. We get the name Elizabeth, then Mr Falker senses sadness and a short temper.

One of the other investigators gets the name Richard. The glass moves.

Were you Mary's lover? Yes. Were you already married? No, and they planned to elope.

By now I can't help myself. Was Mary in danger, I ask. Yes. Did you try and warn her to leave? Yes.

But I already know the story and wonder if I am creating something I want to believe.

Thanet Ghostwatch formed 18 months ago, but some members have been conducting investigations for many years.

"It has been a very good result here," says Mr Falker. "This is one of the few investigations where we have had communication very quickly."

We are about to leave. But a scream comes from the stairway near the top floor. The rest of my

group has discovered a portrait of a Michael Russell, Agent Victualler in 1755 and 1762. Could it be our spirit Michael?

It is freaky, but it hinges on belief. Whether anyone spoke to us, how Mr Falker got the name Michael, why did the trigger objects not move in front of us. All unanswered questions, but a good night out nonetheless.

■ The spooky cellar at Maison Dieu House leads to secret tunnels

WE'RE NOT ALONE

OTHER teams found similar experiences to us.

Like us, the council's allotments officer, Tracey Hubbard, also felt there were five spirits in the building. Her team got the names Michael, Mary, Elizabeth, Roger and Claire.

■ The Thanet Ghostwatch team before the investigation gets under way

Maison Dieu House, report on the Mary Gray investigation by Thanet Ghostwatch Team. (Dover Mercury, 4 April 2007)

the Castle. In the name of William III they took possession of the fortress remaining there all night. In the morning Captain Stokes went up to the gate telling them that due to the strong easterly wind, William of Orange had continued to sail westwards. The men rejoiced, adding that they would only 'yield the Castle to the representative of the new King.' William III made landfall on 5 November in Torbay. The Glorious Revolution that followed was almost bloodless and Mary's heroic action quickly passed into Dover's folklore. Sightings of her ghost were well-documented and she was always seen in the area where she was killed. However, although the legend was based on fact, at the time these events took place both Thomas Papillon and Robert Jacob were in exile in Holland. After the Glorious Revolution, Thomas returned to represent the town in Parliament at the same time as Captain Stokes was again elected Mayor. William III's representative eventually relieved the men holding the Castle and all were offered fitting posts in the army and navy.

Maison Dieu House remained the Agent Victualler's office until 1831, when the house became the home of the Commander of the Royal Engineers in Dover. It was sold in 1834 as a private residence and became the home of William Kingsford of the brewing and milling family. Shortly afterwards, he was declared bankrupt and a year later William Mummery, the owner of Dover's Tannery and three times Mayor of Dover, moved in. His son, Albert Mummery, the father of modern mountaineering, was born there. The house was bought by the Corporation in 1899, and became the offices of the Borough Engineer and Medical Officer of Health. The electricity generating station owned by the council was just round the corner in Park Street, and in 1904 the Medical Officer moved out in

Maison Dieu House today, now occupied by Dover Town Council. (Photo by Alan Sencicle)

Town Clerk's Office, Maison Dieu House, which now includes the site where Mary was killed. (Courtesy of Dover Town Council – photo by Alan Sencicle)

order to provide office space for the electricity station staff. During the Second World War, Maison Dieu House was damaged by enemy action but was repaired following the war and in 1952 became the home of the Dover Public Library. The Library moved to the Dover Discovery Centre's premises in Market Square in 2003. It was while they were preparing to move that I came across Mary's story and before writing it up, I asked one of the librarians if he knew of her ghost? The reply came without any hesitation; Mary had spooked most of the staff and was always found in the same room! The following year Dover Town Council purchased Maison Dieu House for £300,000, gutted and refurbished it.

In 2006, my husband and I had reason to see the Town Mayor and Town Clerk to discuss something over which the latter and we held opposing views. Throughout the discussion, every time the Town Clerk spoke a chime would start, 'dong-dong-ding!' It would stop if either of us spoke and also if the Mayor agreed with us. When the Mayor did not, the 'dong-dong-ding' would start again! The poor Town Clerk soon became very frustrated and said that this was not the first occasion that the 'dong-dong-ding' had happened. He added that the bell had been checked but no fault had been found. Mary's story, by this time, had been published in the *Dover Mercury*, so was well-known. I suggested that it could be Mary, especially as the Town Clerk's new office had been extended to include the exact location of the room where Mary died. At this, the peel of 'dong-dong-ding' went on for well over a minute!

On 4 April 2007 the Thanet Ghostwatch team carried out an investigation into Mary's existence. They confirmed that Mary Gray does haunt Maison Dieu House and a reporter who was with them had a conversation with her. Their further investigations revealed that several other ghosts haunted the house, but it is Mary who was the most prominent ghost.

The Lay of the Old Woman Clothed in Grey — Ingoldsby's Legend of Dover

Biggin Street

Within days of Mary Gray's death at Maison Dieu House in 1688, there were reported sightings of her ghost. Over time she became quite famous and accrued many myths around her appearances. Then in the middle of the nineteenth century Mary's appearances were attributed to another 'ghost' and Mary's story was forgotten. The new character had featured in the then highly popular *Ingoldsby Legends*. Written by the Reverend Richard Harris Barham, the legends are a series of humorous and farcical stories in both prose and verse and set in East Kent. Born in Canterbury, Barham was descended from Sir FitzUrze, one of Thomas Becket's assassins. Although intended for the bar, he took orders in 1813, and four years later became Vicar of Snargate, near Appledore, Kent. In 1821 Barham obtained a minor canon in St Paul's, London, and later held the appointment of Divinity Lecturer at Canterbury Cathedral. However, he is mainly remembered for the *Ingoldsby Legends*, which he wrote under the nom-de-plume Thomas Ingoldsby. First published in *Bentley's Magazine*, the proprietor of which was an old school friend of Barham's, collectively the Legends were published in 1840. A second and third series were added in 1847, under the editorship of the author's son. Richard Barham died in 1844 of a severe cold, caught at the opening of the Royal Exchange. Barham only wrote one story set in Dover; *The Lay of the Old Woman in Grey*.

The tale is about an old woman who, on her deathbed, requests a 'bandy-legged tailor' to go to the nearest convent and ask for Father Basil, so that she can make her final confession. Although the old woman promised to pay the tailor for his errand, she refused when he returned with Father Basil. After making her confession, the old woman died but was then full of remorse for cheating the poor tailor. According to Barham the old woman haunts a Biggin Street shop cellar with a bag of gold. This she wishes to give to the poor tailor or anyone else on his behalf. Although it was Maison Dieu House that it was generally believed the old woman haunted, Barham told his readers to go to Biggin Street:

> You'll be sure to find out if you ask the baker's,
> Then go down with a light
> To the cellar at night;

However:

> ... as soon as you see her don't be in a fright,
> But ask the old hag
> At once for the bag
> If you find that she's shy,
> Or your senses would dazzle,
> Say Ma'am, I insist,
> In the name of St Basil.
> If she gives it you seize
> It and do as you please.

Biggin Street bakers, early twentieth century, one of the supposed haunts of the 'Old Woman in Grey'. (Courtesy of Dover Library)

By the end of the nineteenth century the hunt for the old woman's ghost had become a favourite pastime for those who actually read the clues. Indeed, John Bavington Jones, the nineteenth-century Dover historian, suggested that she could be found at 13 Biggin Street. He goes on to say in his book, Perambulation of Dover that 'a Mr Burkett's had a bakery at that address which had been in his family for more than half a century. Prior to that a William Wood had a bakery on the site.' (p 102–103). William Burkett, of the bakery, was Mayor of Dover in 1905–06 and the site of his shop is approximately where Store 21 and Argos are today. Another favoured site was the Central Bakeries, which stood on the corner of Biggin Street, roughly where Thomas Cook's is today. Albeit, except for Maison Dieu House, which was probably Mary Gray, the sightings of Barham's old woman were rare. This is not surprising as Richard Barham actually acknowledged that he adapted the Dover story from a legend of Boxworth, near St Ives, Cambridgeshire!

The Buckland House Urchin

Buckland House, Crabble Hill

Ghosts of children are not very common in Dover, which makes Jack, who features in this story, extra special. If Buckland House, where Jack resides, was occupied he would probably be seen regularly but it has stood empty since 2000. Nonetheless, like Adele in Cannon Street, Jack is still heard singing and also like Adele, he is most likely to be wearing blue.

For centuries the three-mile long River Dour supported five paper mills. The largest, Buckland Paper Mill on Crabble Hill (the old London Road), made the internationally

Buckland House, where Jack haunts. (Courtesy of Dover Museum)

famous Conqueror paper. Sadly, under the ownership of Arjo Wiggins Teape, the mill closed in 2000. At the time of writing, the buildings have either been bulldozed into oblivion or they stand gaunt and derelict with redevelopment long-promised. Buckland House was part of the mill complex and although prior to closure the site had numerous resident ghosts, as the house is still standing and the singing has been heard, I am just focusing on Jack's story.

I first came across Jack when I was researching my book, *Banking on Dover*, which tells the story of Dover's banking families, including the Minet-Fectors. Peter Fector, who developed the bank that eventually incorporated and then took his surname, had two sons, and one of his granddaughters by his younger son, James, was Emma. In 1822, according to the story of the Buckland House ghost, she married George Dickinson. George was the younger brother of John Dickinson of Croxley, the famous paper maker. John Dickinson, as a wedding present, leased Buckland Paper Mill for his younger brother who, at twenty-nine, was described as 'an awkward, difficult and loutish youth'.

Paper had been made at the Buckland Mill at least since 1638. By 1746 the mill was owned by Thomas Horn who bequeathed it to his sons, Ingram and Thomas. At the time, it was leased from the Church until the brothers bought it in 1788. A disastrous fire in 1814 led to the rebuilding of the mill four years later. Then two years after that it was put up for auction as Thomas Horn wished to retire. When John Dickinson purchased the mill it was known as Buckland Cottage Paper Mill. A year later, in 1821, Buckland House was built.

Following their wedding, according to the story, George and Emma moved into Buckland House. From the start Emma, it was said, was determined to 'polish' her new husband and turn him into a 'a highly thought of member of Dover's society'. She tackled the job with typical Fector determination, including arranging a series of musical soirées. These soon became the talk of the town, which had, and still has, an excellent musical reputation.

Buckland Paper Mill from the Churchyard.   Drawn by T. Fornet, 1770.
Copied from the Original by permission of Mrs. John Horday.
Photo by W. H. Clarkson.

Buckland Paper Mill, 1770. (Courtesy of Dover Museum)

Buckland Paper Mill rag-sorters, late nineteenth century. (Courtesy of B.J.H. Bush)

At that time, and for much of the succeeding century, the paper was made from rags. Rag and bone men would travel through towns and villages collecting old clothes in exchange for sundry items of little use or value but of fascination to children. The rags would then be sold to paper mills, where they would be sorted. Buttons and other such objects were removed and the material would then be soaked in huge vats before being processed into paper. Bones that the rag and bone men also collected would be boiled for making glue. At Buckland Mill, at the time of the story, women and children coming from the local community, including the River Union Workhouse, sorted the rags.

One particular inmate of the workhouse was Jack, an orphan who was both angelic in looks and temperament. All the rag-sorters, including the male overseers, were fond of Jack. Not only did he have a placid nature, he also had an exceptionally beautiful voice and a good memory for songs. Jack's repertoire included popular folksongs, hymns and operatic arias that he heard sung through the open windows of the big houses around Dover. The overseers found that by encouraging Jack to sing, the rag-sorters, instead of spending time in idle gossip, would happily get on with their work, just joining in with the chorus. It was not long before Emma heard about Jack and invited him up to Buckland House to hear him sing. She accompanied the little lad on her pianoforte and was very pleased by his performance. She therefore arranged for Jack to live in the servant's quarters on the top floor of the house and had him cleaned up and measured for some very becoming blue suits. Not satisfied with that, she also paid for Jack to be instructed in basic etiquette and schooling, as well as singing instruction. Emma then held a musical evening where Jack sang to the elite of Dover's society and he was a sensation! Soon he was in demand throughout East Kent. However, Jack, who looked younger than his years, was growing up so his voice began to break. Emma sent to London for one of the best voice coaches in the country, but even he could not salvage Jack's once beautiful

Buckland House staircase where Jack's ghost is most often seen. (Photo by Alan Sencicle)

Buckland Paper Mill post-war. (Courtesy of Dover Museum)

soprano voice. Initially, Emma decided to have Jack trained for domestic duties, but Jack hated them and longed to return to his friends at the mill.

Eventually, Jack was sent back to the workhouse where his old friends made him welcome. He also returned to the mill and as his voice remained pleasant and his repertoire had increased considerably, Jack was soon serenading the rag-sorters as he had done before. Having lived in relative luxury for some time, Jack succumbed to disease, and ceased singing and just swept floors between paroxysms of coughing. One day Jack collapsed and had to be carried back to the workhouse. Hearing that Jack was sick, Emma, full of remorse for not taking better care of her prodigy, took him back to Buckland House. There, it was said, she nursed him herself but it was too late and Jack died. Afterwards, it was said that Jack haunted Buckland House and in an effort to exorcise him, Emma selflessly devoted herself to looking after the needs of the poor of the town. This included helping to instigate and found Dover's hospital, which opened in 1850.

In fact, Emma Fector's husband was not George Dickinson, nor did she live at Buckland House. Emma married William Rastall Dickenson on 25 October 1814 at St James Church, Dover. William was both a Councillor and an Alderman, but the couple were well-known for their musical soirees. Thomas Horn built Buckland House for his retirement and the 1841 census gives Ann Horn as the occupant. George Dickinson never married and in 1837 was also declared bankrupt by the Fector bank. He died of alcoholism in 1843, by which time Buckland House was said to be haunted by a boy in blue with a beautiful voice. Further, the older women working in the rag-sorting shed at the adjacent mill were also recounting the story of Jack. In John Bavington Jones's book on Dover's history, he muddled William Rastall Dickenson with George Dickinson, which is a possible explanation for Jack being given as Emma Fector's protégé. Nonetheless, by the twentieth century Jack's story had passed into local folklore, supported by frequent sightings and hearing him sing. During the Second World War the Observer Corps requisitioned Buckland House and they too regularly reported sightings and hearing Jack. Following the war, like many of Dover's ghost stories, Jack's was almost forgotten.

In 2004 I gave a talk to the Wiggins Teape Pensioners Association and finished with the story of Jack. Before the mill's closure Buckland House had been used as offices, and in the audience were people who worked or frequented the building. They were able to describe Jack, remarking on his beautiful voice and his blue suit of the period of this story! Although Buckland House is, at the time of writing, empty, the caretaker tells me that besides hearing Jack sing, he has also seen him coming down the stairs.

The Black Monk of Castlemount

Castlemount Estate, Castlemount Road, Godwin Road and Castle Avenue

The east side of the Dour Valley, below the Castle, was developed in the late nineteenth century as the 'posh' side of town. The Taswell Estate, which includes Taswell Street, Godwin Road and Leyburne Road, was laid out in 1862. Two years later, a start was made on Victoria Park for senior officers of the regiments stationed in Dover. It was here where Sir Winston Churchill had his wartime home when in the town. The majestic crescent is also home to numerous ghosts.

Victoria Park, c.1880, where a number of ghosts reside. (Courtesy of Dover Library)

Landward of Victoria Crescent is the Dover Castle Estate, consisting of Castle Avenue, Park Avenue and Salisbury Road. This was built by Sir William Crundall, (see page 34), who took out a ninety-nine year building lease in 1881. Overlooking the Castle Estate was the palatial Castlemount, built in 1876, and it is within what were its grounds that the next Dover ghost resides. Established by Robert Chignell, Castlemount was a purpose-built high-class preparatory school for boys. Chignell had previously opened a school on part of the site of what was once Dover Priory, at that time a farm and later Dover College public school. He also owned the haunted Westmount, built 1874, further up Folkestone Road and, at the time of writing, being converted into flats. Besides being an entrepreneurial schoolmaster, Chignell was a keen amateur landscape gardener, supervising the design and terracing of both Westmount and Castlemount's extensive gardens. During the building of the terraces at Castlemount, workmen found a British gold armlet of five coils and weighing twelve ounces. At the time it was described as the finest armlet or torque discovered in England and was sent to the British Museum. When Chignell completed his garden, he invited the townsfolk to promenade and so popular was this, it gave the impetus for the creation of Connaught Park that opened in 1883. Chignell also helped to landscape this. However, Chignell eventually left Dover and by 1891 Reverend Thomas Chirol had taken over the school and he ran it for over a decade.

In 1905 the French Government instituted the separation of the Church and the State, which prohibited the official recognition, payments or subsidies of any religious organisation. This led to a large number of religious communities leaving the country and Edward VII invited them to come to Britain. One such group was the *Les Frères des Ecoles Chrétiennes* monks, known locally by the English translation, 'The Brothers of the Christian Schools'. They opened a house in St Margaret's, east of Dover, and in 1911 opened a second house at Castlemount under Reverend Renaud Octave. Both houses were training centres for teachers, and were so successful that young men came from both France and England.

Castlemount with the castle in the background, the old haunt of the Black Monk. (Courtesy of Dover Museum)

On graduation, many went on to teach throughout the world. At the outbreak of the First World War in 1914, the monks left and Castlemount was commandeered by the military for use as a barracks. On 24 December, at 11 a.m., the first aerial bomb to be dropped on the United Kingdom landed in the garden of Mr Terson of nearby Leyburne Road. Lt. Von Prondzynski had flown the plane, and the blast broke an adjoining window and threw the St James Rectory gardener, James Banks, out of a tree! He was only slightly injured. There is a Dover Society plaque nearby. Following the First World War, the monks returned and the school quickly regained its reputation under the guidance of Brother Damien-George.

It was during the inter-war period that the locals started to talk about a Black Monk haunting the extensive tree-covered grounds of Castlemount. The ghost was seen so often and was so disconcerting that tradesmen became reluctant to call after dark. A typical encounter was told to me by Colin Friend whose uncle, Frank Giddens, met the spectre head on! Frank worked as a delivery boy for Hewitt the bakers of Crafford Street in the 1930s. Jack Hewitt, the famous local character who died in 2004, was the son of the baker. Lots would be drawn between the delivery boys as to who would deliver bread to Castlemount and occasionally Frank would be unlucky and have to go. The transaction ritual that all tradesmen had to go through exacerbated the spookiness of the place, but Frank tried hard not to let that get to him. First he rang the bell on the gate at the bottom of the drive. Then he approached the dark, forbidding, building up the steep, tree-lined drive. At the top, he made his way round to the kitchen door at the back. Although the overhanging trees darkened the entrance, Frank tried not to let that worry him. Within the kitchen door was a hatch, which on arrival would suddenly slide open and a voice would ask what the person's business was. Frank would say that he was delivering bread and a robed arm, with a bony hand, reached out through the hatch. Frank would then put the bread on the hand and collect the money within it. Although Frank had never seen the ghostly Black Monk, once the transaction was completed, he would climb on his bicycle and peddle as fast as could back towards the gate and 'safety'. One particular November evening Frank was heading at speed down the winding drive and was beginning to feel relieved as he saw the gate. Suddenly, a monk came out of the bushes and was walking on a collision course towards Frank. The youngster applied his breaks and swerved, but to no avail, he knew that he was going to crash into the monk. However, when he came to a stop the monk was behind him, standing upright! Frank had ridden straight *through* him! Shaken, Frank dismounted and asked the monk if he was all right, but the monk just vanished before his eyes!

At the outbreak of the Second World War the monks left Dover for good although Brother Damien-George was to carry on teaching until he died on 19 January 1970. In 1940 the RAF No. 961 Balloon Squadron commandeered Castlemount as its 'B' Flight HQ for a short time; 'A' Flight HQ was at Dover College. Throughout this time the Black Monk continued to haunt the grounds, causing problems for those on guard. Afterwards, Castlemount was taken over by the Kent County Council and became a Secondary Modern School in 1948. The Black Monk was frequently seen and is said to have been the first to raise the alarm when disaster struck in the early hours of 8 June 1973. Most of the palatial building was gutted by fire, believed to be arson. The school continued in temporary classrooms until a new one was completed in 1977. Eleven years later the school was informed that it was to be closed within three or four years. The following year the highly respected headmaster, Ken Collier, died. During the Christmas holidays Walmer High School was also gutted by fire and subsequently their pupils were bussed to Castlemount. Nonetheless the school still closed in 1991. During all of this time the Black Monk was still regularly seen.

Following the demolition of the school a small housing estate was built and one of the roads is called Monastery Avenue. In 2008 a couple from New Zealand were staying nearby and during the night, the husband woke to see a shadowy figure entering their room. Thinking that it was his wife, he sat up and asked where she had been and if she was all right. At which his wife, who had been dozing besides him, sat bolt upright, grabbed her husband's arm with one hand and covered her mouth with the other, in an effort to stifle a scream. The shadowy figure stayed in the room for several minutes, leaving through a wall! Next day the couple asked about their nocturnal visitor, to be told that it was the Black Monk of Castlemount and not to worry. They later wrote that it was one of the highlights of their visit to the UK!

The New Inn Centurion and George at the White Horse Inn

York Street/New Street and the White Horse Inn, Castle Hill Road
It was once boasted that a person could have a drink every day in one of Dover's public houses and not drink in the same pub twice within a year! It was also said that most were haunted! Having a resident ghost in a pub that was being used for the smuggling trade was a particularly useful way of explaining any unusual noises. Indeed, in *A Tale of Two Cities*, Charles Dickens gives a vivid account of this nocturnal activity:

> The little narrow crooked town of Dover is itself away from the beach, and ran its head into the chalk cliffs, like a marine ostrich. The beach was a desert of heaps of sea and stones tumbling wildly about, and the sea did what it liked, and what it liked was destruction … Small

New Inn, York Street, the residence of the ghostly centurion. (Courtesy of Dover Museum)

tradesmen who did no business whatever, sometimes unaccountably realised large fortunes, and it was remarkable that nobody in the neighbourhood could endure a lamplighter!

One such pub was the New Inn, on the then York Street. It was already established by the 1830s and had a reputation for connections with the smuggling trade. Indeed, an underground tunnel connected the New Inn with another near the Market Square and in between was an extensive catacomb of cellars. It was here that contraband was hidden. Like all smuggling pubs, the landlord boasted that it was haunted…by several ghosts! One of these, he said, was a Roman centurion and that the spectre would appear through the floor and help himself to any drinks standing on the bar! Of all the New Inn's 'ghosts', the centurion stood the test of time and was seen right up to the pub's closure in 1962. In fact, those who had ventured into the cellars said that ghostly legionnaires haunted them too! The pub closed when the Dover Corporation used a compulsory purchase order to make way for the York Street bypass. Work on the York Street bypass did not start for another few years and during excavations the New Dover Group, forerunners of the Dover Society, contacted archaeologist, Brian Philp, of Kent Archaeological Rescue Unit (KARU). They believed that there could be valuable Roman remains under the site. Although this was refuted by the council and eminent archaeologists, KARU uncovered many large and exceptionally well-preserved Roman buildings that made up the *Classis Britannica* fort. They also discovered the Roman Painted House, the best-preserved building of its type north of the Alps, which opened to the public on 12 May 1977. Albeit, most of the Roman remains are now buried under York Street, giving rise to rumours that ghostly Romans haunt the area. This may not be without foundation, for the New Inn, which had for well over a century played host to a ghostly Roman centurion who had his legionnaires in the cellars, was directly above the Roman remains!

Another pub with a resident ghost is Dover's oldest, the White Horse Inn, at the bottom of Castle Hill, close to the ruins of the old St James' Church. It is also the town's oldest residence. Originally it was two cottages in the ancient hamlet of Uphill. These were knocked into one in 1365 to provide a home for the vergers of St James' Church. With the Reformation of 1536, the church retained its parish status but the verger's house was sold. At that time Uphill was separated from the main town by the River Dour, which had two branches – Eastbrook, following the line of the present Maison Dieu Road; and Westbrook, roughly following the course the river runs today. In between, where Castle Street is now situated, was marshland. At the time the sea, at high tide, came as far as the bottom of Uphill and it was here, when the tide was out, that salt-panners earned a living. As time passed and the sea receded, the land was given over to sheep and the wool-combers moved in. Their industry thrived up until the early nineteenth century and their legacy is in the name Woolcomber Street. The wool-combers cottages that once stood there had a reputation for being haunted.

Woolcomber Street, c.1930. The haunted Woolcomber cottages, now gone, are on the left of the photograph behind the ornate urinal. (Courtesy of Dover Library).

White Horse Inn, the oldest residence in Dover with a famous resident called George. (Photo by Alan Sencicle)

During the time of the salt-panners, in 1545, the old St James' verger's house was occupied by Stephen Warde, 'ale tayster to the porte of Dover', a lucrative position collecting import dues. Both Stephen's sons, John and William, were subsequently elected Mayors and William along with his son, Edward, purchased the extremely lucrative contract as Collectors of the Harbour Dues. Their earnings were in excess of £30 a year – a lot of money in those days. The house stayed in the possession of successive 'ale tasters' including a William Smith who eventually turned the house into an inn. From the days of Henry VIII the town's inns and pubs were obliged to display the name of their establishment but what William called his inn is lost in the mists of time. In 1652, when Nicholas Ramsey obtained permission to sell ale and cider, it was called the City of Edinburgh. He had found the name board from a wrecked American freighter on the beach and nailed it over the door! The inn traded under that name for over 250 years. During this time, the City of Edinburgh was used as the meeting place for actors, while its proximity to the sea made the cellars an ideal place for smugglers to hide their contraband. Soon the standard rumour that the inn was haunted was spread! This was exacerbated by the fact that the cellars were deemed as the coldest place in Dover and therefore were used for storing bodies from St James' parish. In hot weather bodies from the adjacent parish of St Mary's were also stored in the cellars!

In 1818 the inn was renamed the White Horse Inn by Thomas Parry and by that time an actual ghost, by the name of George, was in permanent residence. It was said that George was a drowned mariner whose body had been stored in the cellar. During the remainder of the nineteenth century the White Horse changed hands several times, but became the permanent home of the Dover Rowing Club, founded in 1846. Throughout this time

George was seen regularly and was, at one point, the Rowing Club's mascot. Then in 1890 George received national acclaim! At the time the inn was allowed to open at 5 a.m. for passengers of the new coach service between Dover and St Margaret's, east of Dover, that passed by every day except Sunday. It was reported in the national papers that if the landlord was not awake to serve the travellers, George would! The adjacent old St James' Church, during the Second World War, was badly damaged by shellfire and against strong opposition most of it was demolished in 1952–53. The remains, known as the 'Tidy Ruin', have been classified as an ancient monument. Although the White Horse Inn had survived enemy action, Dover Corporation wanted most pre-war buildings demolished in order to rebuild the town anew. Thus, for a time the White Horse Inn was under severe threat too, but luckily, Dover's oldest pub with its occupant, George, survived and both are still flourishing.

The Tragic Tale of Richard Carter and the Ghost of Hougham Church

Samphire Hoe and St Laurence Church, Hougham

In olden days the parish of Hougham, to the west of Dover, was divided into Church Hougham, East Hougham and West Hougham. The latter became part of Dover in 1832. When Kent historian Edward Hasted was writing around 1790, Round Down cliff was part of Hougham. He noted that in the middle of the cliff, 'are two large square rooms cut out of chalk, one within the other, they are called the Coining House, and have a very difficult way to come at them, the cliff here being upwards of 400ft high.' The Coining House caves had been carved to store smuggled goods and long before Hasted's time they

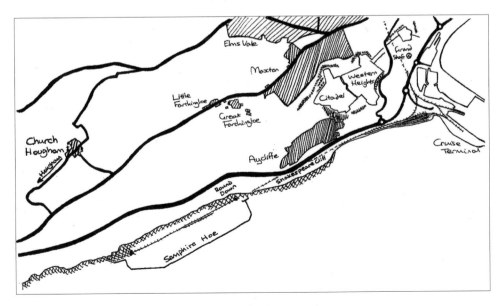

Map showing Samphire Hoe, Hougham and Farthingloe (see page 80).

Round Down Hill, overlooking Samphire Hoe. (Photo by Alan Sencicle)

were known to be haunted by a ghostly voice calling out the name 'Susanne'. This, along with the precarious descent to the caves, served to keep anyone from prying.

The story of Susanne, and the ghost that calls her name, goes back to the middle of the seventeenth century, when English high quality wool was sought after by continental weavers. Wool for export had been smuggled out of the country since 1203 when a tax was first imposed. From 1336 a series of schemes aimed at increasing the royal revenues from wool export were introduced, and with each the illicit trade increased. Over the centuries, customs officers relied heavily on professional informers, who earned their living from the rewards paid on conviction. One such informer was William Carter, a Kent clothier who between 1667 and 1689 was the foremost in the profession and specialised in catching smugglers of unmanufactured wool. Carter's eldest son, Richard, was equal to his father in proficiency. In 1669 Richard came to Dover to investigate a suspected smuggling gang operating between Dover and Hythe. On arrival, he booked into an inn on Limekiln Street in the Pier District of Dover. Within hours of Richard's arrival, word had spread throughout the local community and that evening a particularly attractive young woman, named Susanne, came into the bar. The fact that she looked sad caught Richard's attention and he bought her a drink. She told him that her husband, a sea captain, had gone on a long voyage to the Barbary Coast (North Africa), and that she feared that he had been captured and that she would never see him again. With liberal helpings of ale laced with brandy supplied by the innkeeper, Richard offered Susanne the human warmth she said she craved.

By the next morning, when Susanne left, Richard was in love. Susanne called on Richard the following afternoon and again stayed the night, a routine she maintained over the next

Close-up of Coining House cave that Richard Carter still haunts, calling out for Susanne. (Photo by Alan Sencicle)

few days. Still, Richard could not get enough of her and against her wishes, he followed her one morning. Susanne took the then Folkestone Road along cliff tops. When she arrived at Round Down Cliff, 'a great mist encircled her' and Richard was lost. He eventually found his way back to Dover and that afternoon, Susanne told him that she was aware that he had followed her but begged him not to do so again. Doe-eyed, she reminded the lovesick young man that even though her husband had been missing for over a year, she was still married and that her father, with whom she lived in Hougham, would not approve. Richard agreed, but Susanne ensured his acquiescence by plying him with more drink and love than usual. Next morning, after Susanne left, Richard eventually roused himself and decided to go for a walk over the cliffs to clear his head. As on the day before, when he reached Round Down Cliff the mist came down and he almost stumbled over an iron bar that had been hammered into the cliff. Handling the attached rope, he recognised it as belonging to the samphire gatherers, who precariously collected the plant that grows on the cliff face. At that moment the mist cleared and Richard saw that the rope, instead of going all the way down the cliff face, stopped after about 30ft. Then there was a path that appeared to wend its way down, in a zigzag fashion.

Richard gingerly went down the rope and precariously held onto to the cliff face when he reached the path. Down and down went the path until it eventually led to the huge double cavern, which we know as the Coining House. Inside he saw a large number of sacks and on inspection Richard found that they contained unmanufactured wool. He made a rapid ascent, left a mark near to the samphire gatherers' iron bar and ran as fast as he could back to Dover. On reaching his lodgings Richard was surprised to find his father there but immediately told him of the discovery. Carter, pleased with his son's investigations, left to tell the local customs officials. They consulted with the Mayor, William Stokes, and it was agreed that they would raid the cave that evening. In the afternoon Susanne came to call and Richard told her of the plan. Susanne immediately fell into a faint and on coming to, said that she needed to go home immediately and actually agreed to Richard taking her.

For once it was not misty on Round Down Cliff and as Richard approached the point where he left his mark earlier in the day he saw some men. Suddenly, Susanne recovered her strength and jumped off Richard's horse and ran to them. Confused, Richard dismounted and followed her. He was about to ask Susanne if she was all right when she turned to him, smiled and gave him a hug. Then, with all her strength, she quickly turned them both round and with the help of the men, shoved Richard over the side of the cliff. He fell 400ft (approximately 122 metres) to the beach below. Susanne showed no remorse for her hapless lover, she just smiled cruelly. She then told the smugglers to remove the unmanufactured wool from the cave quickly. By the time Carter and his posse had arrived, Susanne and

Samphire plant that the samphire gatherers once collected and which gave the name to Samphire Hoe. (Courtesy of the White Cliffs Countryside Project)

the smugglers could be seen making their way across the fields towards Hougham church. They gave chase and Carter managed to retrieve forty-four sacks of unmanufactured wool. Two of the smugglers were arrested, John Marsh, Susanne's father, and William Facon of Canterbury. Susanne's husband, it transpired, was a Thomas Pierce and the master of a ship berthed in Dover that was being watched by the customs officials. He was arrested and brought before Mayor William Stokes, who committed him to trial.

Susanne, however, escaped and immediately rode to Folkestone and then on to Hythe, to warn the masters of ships that were involved with the gang there. When Carter reached Folkestone the harbour was empty, but on arrival at Hythe he managed to arrest one sea captain and brought him back to Dover. By that time, Susanne had also returned and gathered a group of women around the town gaol. Armed with pebbles from the beach she compelled Mayor Stokes to let both Pierce and the other master go. However, John Marsh told his captors at Canterbury that his daughter was the brains behind the gang and that her husband was the leader. Susanne's father also implicated his daughter in the murder of Richard. The next morning Richard's body was washed up and a warrant was issued for her arrest, but both she and her husband disappeared. Since then the ghost of Richard has been calling out for Susanne from the Coining House in Round Down Cliff.

In 1994 Samphire Hoe was created out of Channel Tunnel spoil, and from there the Coining House cave can easily be seen. Samphire, after which the Hoe is named, is a succulent plant that grows in crevices on the cliff face and use to be pickled as a delicacy. The samphire gatherers, who drove iron bars into the top of the cliff, attaching a rope which they would climb down to gather the plant, were immortalised by William Shakespeare (1564–1616) in the tragedy *King Lear* (Scene 6, Act 4):

> There is a cliff, whose high and bandy head
> Looks fearfully in the confined deep…
> Show scarce so gross as beetles, halfway down
> Hangs one that gathers samphire, dreadful trade!
> Methinks he seems no bigger than his head.
> The fishermen that walk upon the beach
> Appear like mice…

St Laurence Church, Hougham, before restoration in 1866. (By Lynn Candace Sencicle, adapted from a drawing by J.R. Robbins)

Shakespeare Cliff, between Dover and Round Down Cliff, was named after the play. Today, the White Cliffs Countryside Project (WCCP) looks after the Hoe. Volunteers have reported that on still evenings, a man's voice can be heard coming from the Coining House caves, calling out 'Susanne!'

Over the centuries, following the murder of Richard Carter, smuggling remained a major occupation for the villagers of Hougham. Towards the end of the eighteenth century Thomas Tournay was the parish vicar. He was also the rector of St James Church, Dover, which was next to the White Horse Inn, also known for smuggling at the time. On Reverend Tournay's death in 1795, his son William became Hougham's vicar. It was believed that the Tournays discreetly supported smuggling and local tradition said that the base of the pulpit of St Laurence Church at Church Hougham was used as a receptacle to hide smuggled goods.

Following the death of Reverend William Tournay in 1833, the attitude of the incumbents of St Laurence changed and many of the parishioners took heed, including John Buckle, a farm labourer. Indeed, John was convinced that a ghost, which was reputed to haunt the churchyard, was no more than a cover for smugglers. So strong was his conviction that he contacted the recently formed Coastguard, who asked John to spy for them and even armed him with a pistol. For the next few nights John waited in the churchyard, but nothing happened so he gave up. Then, one December night, he and his friends were walking past the church when they heard a strange sound. John's friends started to run, but he stood his ground, and with caution the others returned. Suddenly a loud droning voice could be heard coming from behind a tombstone and, much to all their dismay, a white clad figure confronted them for a moment and suddenly vanished! All of the men bolted but when John reached his home, he collected the pistol and returned to the churchyard. The ghost immediately rose up and again started to groan. With great trepidation and not

St Laurence Church, Hougham, where signs of contraband were found during restoration. (By Lynn Candace Sencicle, adapted from a drawing by Joseph Mersender)

looking where he was firing, John pressed the trigger. There was a shriek and John took to his heels and ran home, throwing the pistol into a ditch on the way. Next morning, the body of Jeremiah Hales, a well-known smuggler, was found by a gravestone and he was wearing a white sheet. Under the gravestone were kegs of spirit. John owned up to killing Hales and was arrested and sent for trial at Maidstone Assizes. According to an 1840 local newspaper, John Buckle was tried for the murder of Jeremiah Hales but was acquitted. On release, John joined the Coastguards and was based at Hougham.

It is generally believed that the St Laurence Church we see today is a testimony to Robert de Hougham, a Crusader who fought with Richard I in the Third Crusade. In fact major restoration took place in 1866, and the tower was added. At the time, hidden among the rafters, within the pulpit, the font, and numerous other places, the restorers found copious evidence that contraband had been hidden there!

The First Attempt at a Channel Tunnel, Coal, French Invasion and the Ghostly Legacies

Samphire Hoe and Alkham Valley

Samphire Hoe, as we read in the last chapter, was created out of spoil from the Channel Tunnel. Wildflowers and grasses were sown and the resulting vegetation has attracted much wildlife. In 1994 the site was officially named and the White Cliffs Countryside Project (WCCP) now runs this very popular visitor attraction. The Hoe also has its fair share of ghosts! There is Richard Carter, who calls out from the Coining House caves that overlook the Hoe. The WCCP volunteers tell me of a white figure that runs across the

Samphire Hoe. (Photo by Alan Sencicle)

Hoe and into the cliff, which, as it passes by, turns you cold! They also speak of ghostly marching, a phenomenon that has been reported many times since the latter part of the nineteenth century and said to be the footfalls of the original Channel Tunnel workers or Shakespeare Colliery sinkers.

The long history of a channel tunnel began in 1802 when a French mining engineer, Albert Mathieu, put forward an idea linking France and Britain via a tunnel. Surfacing on an artificial island built around the Varne sandbank, the tunnel was then to go underground again, surfacing in Dover, possibly in the Alkham Valley. Although unrealistic in design, when hostilities broke out between France and England a year later, Napoleon gave his approval. This not only had the effect of dogging any channel tunnel projects thereafter through fear of invasion, but left a ghostly legacy that is still reported today!

Towards the end of the nineteenth century a channel tunnel project was started at the foot of Shakespeare Cliff, next to Round Down Cliff. Financed by Edward Watkin, the Chairman of the South Eastern Railway, a 22.55 metre shaft was sunk and a level heading driven for 792.68 metres. A second heading was driven for 1,944 metres under the sea. However, in July 1883 a Joint Committee of both Houses of Parliament held an enquiry into the proposed tunnel and declared that, 'The majority of the Committee are of the opinion that it is not expedient that Parliamentary sanction should be given to a submarine communication between England and France.' The tunnel was abandoned, but soon gained the reputation of being haunted.

As coal had been found across the Channel near Calais, not long after the channel tunnel operations were suspended, a borehole was sunk at the bottom of the abandoned shaft. Coal was found at a depth of just over 300 metres and under the supervision of

Original Channel Tunnel shaft, Shakespeare Cliff, 1880s. (Courtesy of Dover Library)

Inscriptions made by Channel Tunnel workers in 1880. (Courtesy of White Cliffs Countryside Project)

Francis Brady, the Chief Engineer of the Railway Company, drilling was started. In 1896, Arthur Burr formed the Kent Coalfield Syndicate, bought the mineral rights and the first shaft, named after Francis Brady at the new Shakespeare Colliery, was sunk that year.

From the outset the colliery had troubles. A few days after sinking began, Yorkshireman Harry Ball was killed by a chalk fall – Kent coalfield's first mining accident. Due to shortage of money, neither pumps nor pump engine were installed and by 16 October the water level in the pit had reached 112 metres. A second shaft was started, Simpson Pit, and initially this one augured well as it proved to be both dry and without incident. That was until 8.55 p.m. on 6 March 1897, when the bottom of the shaft broke open and water rushed in. At the time, fourteen sinkers were digging, of which six managed to climb to the hoist

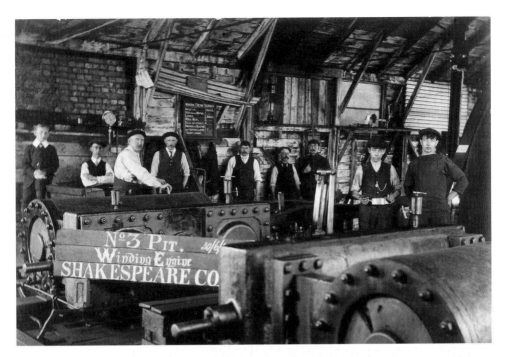

Shakespeare Colliery workers. (Courtesy of White Cliffs Countryside Project)

bucket and were rescued. They then went back into the now waterlogged shaft to try and save their colleagues but to no avail. The eight who lost their lives were Charles Bishop, twenty-eight, of Dover who left a widow and two children; George Terry, twenty-two, also of Dover; John Jarvis Barrs, twenty-two, of Nottinghamshire; Richard Brockwell, twenty-two, of Shropshire; Robert Reed, fifty-four, of Rochester; George Wigman, thirty-six, of Woking, Surrey, married with two children; Samuel Wilmot, thirty-eight, of Derbyshire, married with two children. The eighth man was not named. In 1909, Shakespeare Colliery was placed in the hands of the Receiver and finally abandoned in December 1915 due to poor productivity. After that the site was deemed as being cursed and there were repeated reports from people saying that they could hearing the sounds of marching boots on the shingle. The sound was similar to the crunching sound that the channel tunnellers' or colliery shaft-sinkers' boots made on their way to and from work. It is this ghostly marching that is still being heard today.

At about the time of the Shakespeare Colliery disaster, a High Court case was being heard in London, involving Messrs Banks, Dawes and Sladen. Both of the events received national headlines but the result of the court case led to the selling of the Bushy Ruff Estate in the Alkham Valley and its 478 acres. This included Chilton Farm, where it had been suggested that the original Napoleonic channel tunnel would surface. Whether it was the coincidence of these two events that gave author Max Pemberton the inspiration for his novel *Pro Patriâ*, there is no way of knowing. He was the editor of *Cassell's Magazine*, founder of the London School of Journalism, director of the Northcliffe Newspapers and wrote a number of popular spy stories. *Pro Patriâ*, first published in 1901, describes the preparations for an invasion of England through a channel tunnel. The location of the

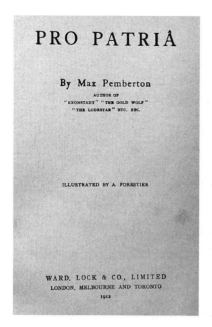

Frontispiece of Pro Patriâ *by Max Pemberton, 1912.*

tunnel exit and the headquarters of the French invasion party are given as 'River Bottom Farm', but this was generally believed to be a pseudonym for Chilton Farm.

Even though the Shakespeare Colliery had proved unproductive, the continual demand for coal encouraged other borings to be undertaken in and around the Dover area. A total of fourteen coal seams, stretching from Dover almost to Herne Bay, were eventually found. One of these borings was at Ellinge, five miles north-west of Dover along the Alkham Valley. The French company undertaking the explorations were optimistic but the editor of the *Dover Express* wrote:

> Mr Max Pemberton's little scare about a French invasion at Chilton, will probably take a more acute form now that a French company is actually preparing to bore and to sink shafts for iron and coal at Ellinge.

The result was that the French company were ordered to cease their operations by the British government! Albeit, the British Companies were allowed to carry on and the first bucketful of commercial East Kent coal was raised at Snowdown Colliery, north of Dover, on 19 November 1912. It had been envisaged to sink fifteen mines, but in the event only three more were opened these were Tilmanstone in 1906, Chislet in 1913 and Betteshanger in 1924. In 1969, Chislet Colliery was closed, both Tilmanstone and Snowdown closed in 1987 and Betteshanger Colliery on 28 August 1989. At Ellinge, the estate continued to be farmed, as it had been for at least two centuries and continued to be so until 1963. A farmhouse was built at the beginning of the nineteenth century but was sold as a private residence in the 1920s. The surrounding area remains agricultural.

As for an invasion through a channel tunnel, during the First World War Dover played a prominent role in defence, and in the Second World War was in the front line when invasion threatened in 1940. In May 1941 Lord Hankey, Chairman of the War Cabinet's

Ellinge House. (Courtesy of Barry and Margaret Sheppard)

Alkham village, 1903. On the road between the village and Dover the ghosts of the Napoleonic horsemen are seen. (Courtesy of Dover Library)

Scientific Advisory Committee, suggested that the Germans had the ability to build a channel tunnel and invade the country that way. The following year an order was issued to all Allied planes and ships in the Dover Strait to keep a look out for discoloration of the sea caused by the building of this suspected tunnel. This proved to be unfounded and in 1994 the Channel Tunnel, we know today, opened. Since then, stories of possible invasion and terrorism have continued to make the headlines. However, in Alkham Valley, along the road near Chilton Farm, such invasion has already taken place. It is here where ghostly Frenchmen on horseback, who are said to have invaded the country by a tunnel during the Napoleonic Wars, are seen!

The Lovers of Ghost Hill, Temple Ewell

Ghost Hill, Temple Ewell

Not far from the Alkham Valley is the village of Temple Ewell, so-called after the Knights Templar (see page 17), who built a house there in the twelfth century. It was not until the eighteenth century that the main road from Dover to London ran through the village, and the present A2 replaced this in 1977. Surrounding Temple Ewell are high, steep hills, one of which is called Ghost Hill after the ghost of a good-looking young man, riding a horse and carrying an older female ghost, pillion fashion.

Their story goes back to 1777, when the American colonies declared their independence. Although the colonists had at first suffered serious setbacks, by October of that year, the situation was beginning to change. They had surrounded the British, under General Burgoyne (after whom Fort Burgoyne and Heights, east of Dover, were named), and forced him to surrender. Up until that time, Louis XVI of France had appeared to show support for the colonists but had neither committed himself nor provided any aid. If he did, the British knew that their cause would be in jeopardy. Tom was a dispatch rider who, on a December day, had crossed from France to Dover carrying an important consignment. In his satchel was proof that Louis XVI was about to sign a trade agreement with the colonists that would provide the aid they needed. As was Tom's custom, on arrival

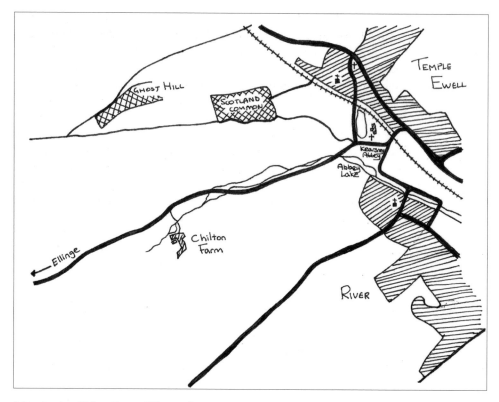

Map showing Chilton Farm, Alkham Valley (see page 68) and Ghost Hill, Temple Ewell.

Ship Hotel, Custom House Quay, c.1834 where Elizabeth Worthington lived. (From an etching by Lynn Candace Sencicle)

in Dover, he rode to the Castle to hand the dispatch on to someone else. He then planned to see his beloved Elizabeth, daughter of Benjamin Worthington, who owned the Ship Hotel on Custom House Quay. The Quay is now the Snargate Street side of the Granville Dock.

However, on arrival at the Castle, Tom was told that the Prime Minister, Frederick, Lord North, Earl of Guilford, was at his country residence of Waldershare, north-east of Dover. Tom agreed to deliver the dispatches directly to the Prime Minister. On reading them, Lord North wrote a letter and instructed Tom to return to the Castle, collect the fastest horse there and ride in haste straight to London. Tom was a little concerned over this, for not only had he hardly eaten or slept since he left Paris two days before, he had promised to meet Elizabeth, who would be worried. Lord North was sympathetic to this and agreed to Tom making a brief detour to see his beloved. The young man returned to the Castle, collected Lightning, the fastest horse in the stable, and soon made his way through the dark, crooked streets of Dover to the Ship Hotel. On arrival Tom was told that the Worthington family were attending a funeral, but were expected back at any time. While waiting for Elizabeth, Tom got into conversation with two customers whom he had seen before at the Hotel. Although he was careful not to say anything about Lord North's letter in Lightning's saddlebag, as time passed Tom became more anxious to be off to London. Noting Tom's agitation, one of the men suggested that he should pass a message on to Elizabeth, while the other offered Tom a 'tot of spirit' to keep out the cold. Tom had no sooner swallowed the drink than he felt his legs go weak and his head spin. The men were French spies and Tom had been drugged!

It was not long after that Elizabeth and her father returned, by which time the men had gone. They managed to rouse Tom sufficiently for him to tell the urgency of delivering Lord North's dispatch to London. Although it was bitterly cold and icy, Elizabeth left Tom in the care of her father in order to take the message herself. Understanding the

Temple Ewell, c.1850 with Ghost Hill behind where Tom and Elizabeth's ghosts are seen. (Courtesy of Dover Library)

urgency of the task, she told her father that she would go through the town, then along the River Dour to Kearsney and Temple Ewell and then over the hills to join the London road. She reasoned that the marshy riverbank would be hard because of the heavy frost. However, Temple Ewell in those days, according to the historian Edward Hasted, was in a very poor state. The houses, he tells us, were, 'little more than cottages, being most of them meanly built of flint, and a great part of them in a very ruinous condition…' As Elizabeth was riding through the village a cloud passed across the moon and Lightning stumbled. Elizabeth was thrown and hit her head against the wall of one of the derelict cottages. Lightning eventually found its way back to the Castle, where the alarm was raised. It was not until the next morning that Elizabeth was found, by which time she was frozen and appeared lifeless. Her father, Benjamin, came to the village, and took Elizabeth home. Tom, having collected the dispatches from Lightning's saddlebag, took another horse from the Castle stable and rode straight to London using the then main road.

Two months later, on 6 February 1778, France openly recognised the American colonists' independence. By that time, thanks to the dispatches Tom had brought over from France and the subsequent letter from Lord North, the government had raised sixteen regiments. The American War of Independence was to last another three years, ending with the French cutting off the British supplies at Yorktown in 1781. Two years later, the British recognised the colonists' independence. As for Tom, exhausted and still suffering from the effects of the drugs, he collapsed in London and never recovered.

The Ship Hotel was listed in the census of 1545 and it is recorded that in 1799 the proprietor was Benjamin Worthington. Ben and his wife Anne had several daughters, one of which was called Elizabeth. According to the baptism records of St Mary's Church, she was born 13 March 1757. This would make her twenty at the time of the story. Elizabeth died in June 1807 and was buried at St Mary's Church. She was fifty years old and had never married. It was said that Tom's ghost returned to Temple Ewell to look for his beloved Elizabeth, whom he believed to be dead. She, after recovery, was frequently seen wandering the hills that surround the village until she too died. Afterwards, the hill where their ghosts are still seen today was aptly named Ghost Hill!

The Cursed William de Malmain

Waldershare Park, Malmain's Wood and the Roads, Lanes and Byways to Dover
For centuries the main road to London was by way of the Castle, then Guston and Whitfield. To the north of Whitfield are Waldershare Park and Malmain's Wood. In the vicinity of Waldershare and along the roads, lanes and byways leading to Dover is the ghost of a distraught middle-aged man on a great steed. His name is William de Malmain and he has been wandering for 800 years looking for a particular young woman to whom he wishes to apologise and put right the wrong he did her.

The first Malmain to come to England was John, who arrived with William the Conqueror and fought at the Battle of Hastings. From him descended several branches of the family who possessed the Kent manors of Pluckley, Alkham, Stoke and Waldershare. The original manor house at Waldershare was Saxon in origin until one of John's descendants, William de Malmain of our story, decided to replace it with a grand new mansion. This was at the

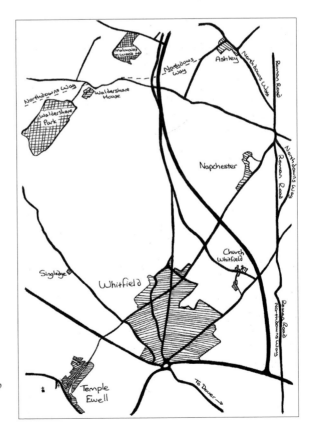

Map showing Malmain's Wood and Waldershare, and the roads leading to Dover where William de Malmain's ghost is usually seen.

beginning of the thirteenth century. One cold winter's afternoon, while riding round his vast estate, Malmain came across a young woman who had been battered and ravaged. While she was being severely assaulted, her three-year-old daughter had run off in terror and the young mother was looking for her. Malmain, against the woman's pleas for help, made to ride off but she made a grab for Malmain's coat. Angrily, he slashed savagely at her with his whip until she eventually let go and he cantered away. The young woman, distressed and still bleeding from the wounds that Malmain had inflicted, carried on searching, continually calling out the child's name. Late into the evening she wandered into the camp where the men who were building Malmain's new mansion lived. She asked for their help but the overseer said that he would have to get Malmain's permission first, otherwise they would be flogged. Malmain was furious at the request, saying that the men needed their sleep in order to be fresh for work the following morning. As for the woman, he ordered that she should be held captive and taken to Dover the following day to be charged with trespass. All night the men were kept awake by the woman calling out her daughter's name from the tiny prison they had locked her in.

The night was bitterly cold and the next morning the men had difficulty undoing the ropes that constrained the woman. As soon as they released her she ran off into the woods, still calling out her daughter's name. Later that morning the young mother found her daughter, frozen to death. She carefully lifted and then wrapped the body in her shawl, and carried it to Malmain's unfinished mansion. There she saw Malmain and set her precious bundle down at his feet. He just walked over the body and ordered one of the men to remove both the dead child and the mother. At this the young mother picked the child up, kissed the cold forehead, looked Malmain straight in the eye and said:

Listen, de Malmain! 'Tis through thee that I hold this lifeless body which but yesterday was my loved and living child. Now she is no more, nor can thou, proud man, call back her flitted spirit. But 'tis thine to pay the price of her little life; thine 'tis to bear the penalty.

Her voice then became loud but solemn,

I say, thou are cursed! Thy child like mine, shall die. Even now she sickens, aye, even now, nor shall she mend, though the King's leech attend her and thy wealth lavish comfort around her bed. And, thy heart broken by thy daughter's loss shalt wander wearily, unloving and unloved forever and nought that though beginnest shall ever be completed.

Awestruck, the men stood and watched as the young woman then tenderly picked up the body of her dead daughter and walked back into the woods. She was never seen again.

As for Malmain, he looked deeply troubled for although he was 'black in his heart and evil in his life,' he did have one soft spot. That was Isabella, his ten-year-old daughter whose mother had died in childbirth. Immediately on hearing the curse, Malmain returned home to find that Isabella had been taken ill. For several weeks the child lingered, but eventually died, even though Malmain had paid for the best medical care in the land. Full of misery and remorse, William de Malmain abandoned the building of his mansion and spent the rest of his days wandering along the tracks between Waldershare and Dover, looking for the young woman to beg her forgiveness. He was buried in St Radigund's Abbey, west of Dover, in 1224.

During his life, William de Malmain probably lived in Malmain Manor, now Malmain's Farm, which does have ancient foundations. His proposed mansion was probably on the site

Malmain's Farm, 1995. Part of the foundations date back to before William de Malmain's time. (Courtesy of Dover Library)

Waldershare Mansion in 1838, rebuilt in the Queen Anne style between 1702–1710. (Courtesy of Dover Library)

of the present Waldershare Park to the south-east of Malmain's farm. John Monins completed this in late medieval times but was replaced by a stately home between 1702-1710. This was in the Queen Anne style with formal gardens. Through marriage the stately mansion came into the hands of Francis, Earl of Guilford, in 1766, who also succeeded to the title of Lord North. His son was Frederick, Lord North, the Prime Minister mentioned in previous stories.

Due to costs and lack of use, half of the great mansion was converted into a chicken house in 1860. Then, on 30 September 1913, it was gutted by fire. Restored again during the Second World War when Dover's Royal Victoria Hospital was requisitioned, Waldershare became the hospital for Dover patients. By 1969, the house was again in need of restoration and was sold but the cost of renovating and conversion was so high that the Earl of Guilford repurchased

Waldershare Park, rebuilt following the fire of 1913. (Courtesy of Dover Museum)

it three years later. He then set about restoring and converting the mansion into luxury apartments. Now it is a Grade I listed country house in 1,760 acres of open woodland and farmland, over which the resident ghost, William de Malmain, still wanders!

The Farthingloe Lady, Sir Gawain and the Eurotunnel Workers Camp

Farthingloe, West of Dover

Darren and Chris had not long been working on the construction of the Channel Tunnel (see page 68), which opened in 1994. Like many other construction workers from outside the area, they lived in the purpose built camp, nicknamed Stalag 15, in Farthingloe Valley to the west of Dover. The camp was made up of some 1,600 rooms in thirty-eight bedroom blocks, but as the two young men were paid on average £1,000 a week, they did not begrudge the £45 for accommodation. Their days were long and hard and time off could be spent in the camp's recreational facilities or going into Dover. This particular evening, in 1991, they chose the latter.

The two aimed to walk down the Folkestone Road, towards Dover, stopping at each pub for a drink until they found one that offered the right sort of company. As they were leaving the camp a woman, her face covered with a light gauze, passed them going in. She was wearing a hooded cloak and underneath a long, loose grey dress. She gave the men a slight curtsy, which they found amusing, and guessed that she was seeing one of their colleagues. However, when they turned back to see which way she went, the woman had disappeared. The first pub Darren and Chris came to was the Hare & Hounds (now closed), where they met up with some of their colleagues. During conversation the two

The former Channel Tunnel Workers Camp in the Farthingloe Valley, where the Lady of Farthingloe was seen. (Courtesy of Dover Museum)

mentioned the woman, remarking that she looked as if she was going to a fancy dress party. They also said that she had disappeared so did not see where she was going. Much to Darren and Chris's surprise, instead of jovial speculation, the other men became serious and said that they too had seen the woman and it was generally thought that she may be a ghost! They then started laughing loudly, and added that they too had seen her and wondered whom she was having an affair with. Listening was a local elderly gentleman, who had lived in nearby Maxton all his life. When the tunnel workers had finished speculating and joking he raised his voice saying, 'Tha's no joke, ya's seen the Lady of Farthingloe. She's been wandering up and down't valley for centuries. Prob'ly the wench is confounded by your huts … but that's who 'tis.' A few of the men sniggered but Darren and Chris wanted to know more.

When I first met Darren and Chris, in the local studies section of Dover Library not long after, they did not say anything about seeing the Lady of Farthingloe. They just told me that they were interested and wanted to know more. I told them that back in the days of the fabled King Arthur there lived in Farthingloe Valley a Lady, whose name was never documented, of great beauty. So great was her beauty that knights travelling to the continent, by way of Dover, would make a detour to the then enclosed valley in order to capture a glimpse of her. It was not until 1762, with the building of the road to Folkestone, did the valley become a thoroughfare. One day, Sir Gawain, King Arthur's nephew and warrior of great repute, having just returned from the continent, was about to give thanks for a safe crossing at the monastery of St Martin-le-Grand. This once stood in Market Square. Coming out of the chapel was the Lady of Farthingloe and he asked the Canons of St Martin's for an introduction. Well known as a ladies' man, they declined. Not to be put off, he made further enquiries, finally he found out where she lived and went to see her. Sir Gawain used all his charm to woo the Lady of Farthingloe and promised to come back, after seeking King Arthur's permission at Camelot, to marry her.

In fact it was another seven years before Sir Gawain returned to Dover and the Lady was seriously ill. Although the Canons were angry at Sir Gawain's behaviour towards the Lady,

The ruins of St Martin-le-Grand, 1792, where 1,000 years before Sir Gawain had first seen the Lady of Farthingloe. (Courtesy of Dover Library)

they were also aware that the knight had a great understanding of herbs. They therefore told him of her illness and asked Sir Gawain to take pity on the Lady. Sir Gawain, thinking that this was a trap, said that he was in a hurry to seek passage to the continent. The Canons begged him to at least see her and make a potion that they could administer. Finally, Sir Gawain agreed but was deeply shocked when he saw the Lady, for she was at death's door. Full of remorse for betraying her trust seven years before, he took over her care. Sir Gawain's devotion even astounded the Canons and eventually the Lady made a good recovery but was 'cruelly pitted'. By this time Sir Gawain was so in love with the Lady, he hardly noticed. As soon as she was well enough they were married and lived in quiet seclusion in the Farthingloe valley. Time passed until one day Sir Gawain's two brothers, Sir Agravain and Sir Mordred, came to stay at Farthingloe. During conversation they told Sir Gawain that the King's beautiful young wife, Queen Guinevere, was having an affair with the handsome Sir Lancelot. They went on to say that on their return to Camelot they planned to tell King Arthur. Up until Sir Gawain settling in Farthingloe, he and Sir Lancelot and been great friends and comrades so Sir Gawain asked his brothers to wait until he had spoken to Sir Lancelot. The next day all three left for Camelot and on arrival, Sir Gawain first paid homage to the King, as was the custom. He then went to see Sir Lancelot, who opened his heart to Sir Gawain declaring his love for Queen Guinevere. Sir Gawain suggested that Sir Lancelot should leave Camelot immediately and come with him to Farthingloe and then consider going back to the continent. Unbeknown to both, Sir Mordred, instead of waiting as Sir Gawain had asked, had seen the King and told him of his wife's indiscretion.

Arthur at first did not want to believe Sir Mordred, so laid a trap for his wife. It was a trap that Queen Guinevere could easily escape, but she did not. Instead she admitted her love for Sir Lancelot and a subsequent Round Table court sentenced the Queen to be burnt at the stake. Sir Gawain had voted against this, but his two brothers were ordered to guard Queen Guinevere until the punishment was executed. On the day sentence was passed, Sir Lancelot had disappeared and Sir Gawain assumed that he had ridden to a port and was on his way to France. However, just as the pyre was about to be lit, Lancelot rode in and managed to free the Queen. It was evident to Sir Gawain that the love that the Queen and

Sir Lancelot shared was similar to the love he had for the Lady of Farthingloe. Then, as the pair were riding out, Sir Gawain saw Sir Lancelot draw his sword and the next second, Sir Lancelot thrust his sword into Sir Agravain. Sir Gawain rushed to defend Sir Mordred, who was also in mortal danger. Between them, they fought off Sir Lancelot, but he was able to make escape with the Queen. Injuries stopped Sir Lancelot from going too far and within hours the Queen allowed herself to be recaptured in order for him to escape. On her return to Camelot, a Round Table was convened and Sir Mordred demanded that the King should gather together his forces and seek out Sir Lancelot. It was agreed that Sir Gawain would go with the King while Sir Mordred would look after the kingdom. Sir Lancelot escaped to France, with King Arthur, Sir Gawain and their men in pursuit. Once Arthur had gone abroad, Sir Mordred proclaimed himself King and released Queen Guinevere, whom he intended to marry. The Queen, however, ran away and sought sanctuary in a convent.

Eventually, without any success in finding Sir Lancelot, King Arthur and Sir Gawain, with their men, returned to England by way of Dover. In Farthingloe valley the King was charmed by the Lady of Farthingloe and invited her to stay at Camelot. Unfortunately, when Sir Mordred had heard of King Arthur's return he sent a rider to inform the King that if he wanted the kingdom he would have to fight for it. Sir Mordred then set out, with his army, and the two sides met on Barham Downs, between Canterbury and Dover. There a bitter battle took place and the Lady of Farthingloe spent the day tending the wounded. As night fell she became increasingly worried about the fate of Sir Gawain, whom she had not seen for several hours. Together with King Arthur, they searched the battlefield but could only find Sir Gawain's head. This she took to St Martin's and the Canons buried it within a silver casket. Following the battle, an uneasy peace returned but only at the expense of King Arthur creating the separate kingdom of Kent. This was to be under the rule of Sir Mordred until the King's death, when Sir Mordred would succeed him.

One night Sir Gawain appeared to the Lady of Farthingloe in a dream, with a message for King Arthur. The story goes that the Lady immediately, 'set forth for Camelot to warn the King of Sir Mordred's impending treachery'. On arrival, because the Lady kept her disfigured face covered, the guards would not allow her to see King Arthur. One of her maids eventually managed to gain an audience and the King summoned the Lady to his presence. She was telling him of the dream when Sir Mordred, who had been listening behind a column, challenged the King. The Lady watched with horror as they both fought to the death. This resulted in a civil war during which Camelot was destroyed and the Dark Ages began. However, the Lady of Farthingloe managed to escape and eventually joined Queen Guinevere in the same convent. Later she gave the Manor of Farthingloe to the Canons of St Martin's.

I went on to tell the two former Channel Tunnel workers that from historic documents we know that Farthingloe was originally called Venson Dane and Wellclose. It belonged, from Saxon times, to the Canons of St Martin-le-Grand. The name Farthingloe originated with Matilda de Ffarninglo, who held the manor in 1385, and it was about this time that the legend was, apparently, first written down. Matilda was reputed to have been a great beauty until she too was disfigured following an illness. As for Sir Gawain, it was believed that following the demise of St Martin-le-Grand in 1136, his skull was removed to St Mary de Castro Church at the Castle. Indeed, in Caxton's preface to Malory's tales, he says, '…in the Castle of Dover ye may see Gawain's skull,' but it has since been lost. Following the dissolution of the monasteries in 1535, Farthingloe passed into the King's hands, who exchanged it in a deal with the Archbishop of Canterbury. During the twentieth century,

St Mary de Castro Church at the Castle, where Sir Gawain's skull was kept. (Courtesy of Dover Library)

the valley came into the hands of the War Ministry, which later became the Ministry of Defence (MoD). Prior to building the Channel Tunnel, Eurotunnel made a bid to buy thirty-six acres of land for a temporary Channel Tunnel work camp at Great Farthingloe farm. It was envisaged that the site would be turned into a business distribution and industrial storage centre, but the MoD had other ideas. Only the temporary workers camp, which cost Eurotunnel £9 million, was built. The camp was empty by 1993 and the contents were put up for auction. Each thirty-eight bedroom block sold for £16,000.

I occasionally saw Darren and Chris afterwards and knew that one, if not both, had settled in Dover and was a volunteer with the White Cliffs Countryside Project. While researching for this anthology, I managed to get in touch with both and asked if they had ever *seen* the Lady of Farthingloe? They became thoughtful, shuffled a bit and then Darren broke the silence. Embarrassed, he told me of their encounter with the Lady of Farthingloe and the conversation with the old gentleman from Maxton. After that night they, and other workers at the camp, had seen the Lady of Farthingloe in the vicinity of 'Stalag 15' several times. When the camp closed, they had expected her to disappear but, they said, she is usually seen about dusk, almost drifting near Folkestone Road, to what had been the entrance to the workers camp, where she disappears!

Jimmy – Lest He Be Forgotten

Cruise Terminal One, the former Marine Station, Western Docks

The final story in this anthology of Dover's ghosts concerns a young man, Jimmy, who has been welcoming passengers to the town's Western Docks for over ninety years. Much-loved, Jimmy was to play an important part in ensuring that the Railway Workers War Memorial, in Cruise Terminal One, Western Docks, stayed there.

Although at the end of the nineteenth century Dover was one of the wealthiest towns in the country, within ten years much of the source of that wealth had gone. The military presence had been severely reduced and the transatlantic liner service had failed. The town council, in conjunction with the Dover Harbour Board – the town's Mayor, William

Crundall, was the Chairman of the Board – in an effort to reverse this trend decided to expand and upgrade the cross-Channel operations. The Admiralty were persuaded to take the east side of the Prince of Wales Pier and they also agreed to widen the Admiralty Pier. At the same time, the South Eastern & Chatham Railway Company obtained a lease to build the grand Marine Station, for the continental boat service.

At the time, there existed a number of defence alliances between the major world powers, supposedly to stop catastrophic conflicts. However, Germany, in order to carry out what was called the Schlieffen Plan, was building up its military strength. It is well documented that on 22 June 1914 a Serbian student assassinated the Austrian Archduke Ferdinand. In accordance with the Schlieffen Plan, on 3 August 1914 Germany declared war on France and massed her troops on the Belgium border. A Treaty of 1839 had given Belgium neutrality and the British demanded that Germany respect it. They refused and the next day Britain declared war and at once mobilised an Expeditionary Force. At the time it was sincerely believed that the Germans would withdraw to within their own frontiers and the war would be over by Christmas. The Expeditionary Force landed in France on 17 August but by then the German troops had routed the Belgian Army. The Expeditionary Force, together with the French Army, met the Germans at Mons on 31 August 1914. There the French were overcome and forced into a full retreat to the Somme and left the city of Antwerp vulnerable. In Britain, this had been watched with avid interest and volunteers were keen to go to Antwerp to help.

One such volunteer was Jimmy, who worked for the South Eastern & Chatham Railway Company. He was sent to Betteshanger training camp, near Deal. On 3 September 1914, the first Lord of the Admiralty, Winston Churchill, decided to send Jimmy's division to help the beleaguered city of Antwerp, but events had moved so fast most of the men lacked training, full uniforms and equipment. Nonetheless, the next day, they marched from Betteshanger to Dover to catch the ferries. They had been reassured that once on the continent they would undergo further training and be fully equipped before advancing to Antwerp. On

THE MARINE STATION AND ADMIRALTY PIER, DOVER

Marine Station and Admiralty Pier, early twentieth century. (Courtesy of Dover Museum)

Early First World War recruiting poster. (Courtesy of the Doyle Collection)

arrival in Dover, Jimmy and his mates were met by the town's band and escorted along the sea front. Crowds had already gathered and they cheered. Jimmy, although lacking a belt to hold up his trousers or a greatcoat, and having no idea how to use a rifle, was proud. Like his mates, he was going off to serve his country. At the Marine Station, along with other former employees of the Railway Company, Jimmy called out to the booking clerks reminding them to keep their jobs open, as they would be back by Christmas. Once on Admiralty Pier, they sat down to wait for the ships to take them across the Channel. It was not until the next day that the ships arrived and the night had been exceptionally cold. Not only were the men inadequately dressed, there was no food for them either.

Eventually, the platoon arrived in France but instead of being provided with further training and adequate clothing and equipment, they went straight to Antwerp. They put up a good fight, but the city fell and remained occupied until 1918. Most of the survivors from Jimmy's contingency were taken prisoner, but some managed to escape and make for England. Jimmy was one, and they eventually arrived in Dover on 12 October. In contrast to the embarkation, they were treated as an embarrassment and were taken straight to Betteshanger. They did not stay there long before returning to the Continent. Jimmy was on the Somme when the month-long battle began on 1 July 1916. The Anglo-French armies attempted to break through German lines with a massive infantry assault. They had been told that the barbed wire would be cut, and most of the enemy killed, before the attack. The confidence of the British and Allies was summed up by Captain Wilfred 'Billy' Neville, an old boy of Dover College, who likened the proposed offensive to a game of football – he even issued his men with footballs!

The first day is still seen as the blackest day in the history of the British Army when there were 57,470 casualties of which 21,000 died, most in the first thirty minutes of the assault.

First World War troop movement – Admiralty Pier. (Courtesy of Dover Museum)

Both Captain Neville and Jimmy were mowed down in a hail of bullets. By the end of the month, there were 600,000 casualties, two-thirds of which were British. The Buffs (East Kent Regiment) sustained over 1,000 casualties and as Dover was the main base for ambulance ships, many of the wounded returned through Marine Station. It was about this time that the ghost of Jimmy was first seen, wearing a tattered combat uniform on Admiralty Pier, waving to those going to the Western Front. He also greeted the injured who returned. Between 1915 and the end of the war in 1918, more than 1.2 million wounded men were landed on Admiralty Pier, with up to twenty ambulance trains a day leaving the Marine Station.

Following the end of hostilities the station was eventually opened up for civilian use in January 1919. On 10 November 1920, the body of the Unknown Warrior arrived on the *Verdun*, at what is now Cruise Terminal One, before being taken to Westminster Abbey. There is a plaque to mark the landing. In 1922, the Railway Workers' Memorial, designed by W.C.H. King, was unveiled within Marine Station. It is a bronze figure of Victory flanked by a soldier, a sailor, and behind them, a bugler playing the 'Last Post'. The inscription reads: 'To the Immortal memory of the 556 men of the South Eastern and Chatham Railway who fought and died for their country in the Great War 1914–1918'. It then lists the departments where they had worked.

Under the Railways Act of 1921, the South Eastern & Chatham Railway Company amalgamated with other companies to form Southern Railway. On 15 May 1929, Southern Railway launched its 'super-class travel' from London to the continent. Called the Golden Arrow service it used the specially built ferry, *Canterbury*, to carry passengers, in their coaches, across the Channel. Using the Admiralty Pier, the service continued up until the outbreak of the Second World War and was reintroduced following the war. In the 1920s, James Ryland

Unveiling of the Railway Workers' Memorial, 1922. (Courtesy of Dover Library)

of George Hammond persuaded cruise liners to call at Dover again. The Royal Netherlands Steamship Company's *Simon Bolivar* called in 1927 on her maiden voyage. She was sunk on 18 November 1939 when she hit a mine off Harwich. In 1932 the *Umkuzi* called at the port, and the following year the Horn Line made Dover a regular port of call. Picking up passengers from London arriving at Marine Station, the ships, which had come from Hamburg, took passengers to Trinidad. The Norddeutscher Line also used the port for its Far Eastern destinations and the Holland African Line often used the port. Many of the well-to-do passengers of these cruise liners complained of the 'beggar' wearing a tattered old uniform who hung about the Marine Station, but most were appeased when they were told that the 'beggar' was Jimmy's ghost. Passengers travelling regularly through the port then made a special point of looking out for Jimmy such that he became a minor celebrity, making the national newspapers.

The Marine Station was again pressed into military service at the outbreak of the Second World War. During the 1940 Dunkirk evacuation nearly 200,000 British and Allied troops were landed on Admiralty Pier and transported out from Marine Station. Jimmy was there to wave goodbye or to greet them all and as such became a popular 'mascot'. Like much of Dover, the station suffered badly from war damage, including a bomb penetrating the roof, causing a large crater. Following the war the station was renovated and the Southern Railway were running services again. Another plaque was then added to the war memorial saying, 'And to the 626 men of the Southern Railway who gave their lives in the 1939–1945 war'. Jimmy, was mainly seen next to the Memorial.

In 1992 the lease expired on Marine Station and there were a number of proposals as to what should be done with the Railway Workers' War Memorial. British Rail wanted to move the Memorial to the town's main station, the Priory, but a public outcry stopped that. One of the arguments given against the removal of the Memorial was Jimmy and it was feared that he would be left behind, and what he represented would be forgotten. 1994 saw the opening of the Channel Tunnel that threatened the future of the ferry industry in Dover and the Dover Harbour Board responded by once again attracting cruise liners to Dover. They also took over the old Station to provide a cruise terminal. The Harbour Board spent some £10m restoring Marine station, a Grade II listed building. Due to its listed status, the railway tracks had to be retained and are beneath the inside parking area! Thus the Railway Workers' War Memorial, together with Jimmy, stayed. He is still seen today, wearing his tattered uniform, in the vicinity of the Memorial, much to the bemusement of cruise passengers.

Bomb damaged Marine Station , Second World War. (Courtesy of Dover Library)

The Railway Workers' Memorial, near which Jimmy is mainly seen. (Courtesy of Dover Harbour Board)

BIBLIOGRAPHY AND SUGGESTED READING

Barham, Richard Harris (1840): *Ingoldsby Legends*. (Reprinted Odham's Press Ltd 1930)

Batcheller, W. (1828, 1844, 1845, 1865): *History of Dover*

Dover Chronicle: Various

Dover Express: Various

Dover Telegraph: Various

East Kent Mercury: Various

Haines, Charles Reginald (1930): *Dover Priory*. (Cambridge University Press)

Harman, Joe: Various articles published in the *Dover Mercury*

Hasted, Edward (1799): *History of the County of Kent*

Horsley, M.: *Some Memories of Old Dover*

Horsley, M.: *Some More Memories of Old Dover*

Ireland, W.H. (1829): *England's Topographer or A new and Complete History of Kent*. (G. Virtue)

Jones, John Bavington (1916): *Annals of Dover*. (Dover Express Printworks)

Jones, John Bavington (1907): *A Perambulation of the Town, Port, and Fortress of Dover*.

Jones, John Bavington (1920): *Records of Dover*

Knocker, Edward (1878): *The Archives of Dover*. (Standard)

William, Lombarde: (1576): *Perambulation of Kent*. (Reprinted in 1970 by Bath, Adams and Dart)

Lyon, Reverend (1813): *The History of the Town and Port of Dover* [Vol. I & II] (Revised Clarendon Press)

Page, William (Ed.), (1974): *Victoria History of the Counties of England – Kent*. (Dawsons of Pall Mall)

Pattenden, Thomas (1797–1819): *Diaries Volume 1–4*. (Dover Library microfiche)

Pemberton, Max (1912): *Pro Patriâ*. (Ward, Lock & Co. Ltd)

Pigot Guide Books: Various editions

Sencicle, Lorraine (1994): Banking on Dover.

Sencicle, Lorraine: Articles published in the *Dover Mercury*, (Kent Messenger Group).

Smith, Barry (1978): *By the Way – Dover's Pubs*

Statham, Reverend S.P.H. (1899): *The History of the Castle, Town and Port of Dover*. (Longmans, Green & Co.)

INDEX

Other titles published by The History Press

Haunted Kent

JANET CAMERON

Contained in this selection are stories of the hunchback monk at Boughton Malherbe, the black dog of Leeds, Canterbury's faithless friar and Dungeness' mysterious lady, as well as the famous tale of Lady Blanche of Rochester Castle. This fascinating collection of strange sightings and happenings in the county's streets, churches, public houses and country lanes is sure to appeal to anyone wondering why Kent is known as the most haunted county in England.

978 0 7524 3605 8

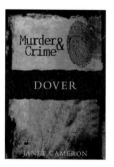

Murder & Crime Dover

JANET CAMERON

Those who fell foul of the law in Kent faced a horrible fate: some were thrown to their deaths from the top of Dover's iconic white cliffs, whilst others were hanged, quartered, burnt or buried alive. Yet still the criminal fraternity of Kent went undeterred. This fascinating book contains tales of thwarted rivals and wicked soldiers, desperate mothers, licentious monks and disreputable women. With more than fifty illustrations, this chilling catalogue of murderous misdeeds is bound to captivate anyone interested in the criminal history of the area.

978 0 7524 3978 5

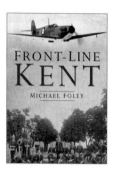

Front-Line Kent

MICHAEL FOLEY

Kent has been on England's first line of defence. Many people in the county have lived closer to the enemy in Europe than they did to London. This book delves into the long history of military Kent, from Roman forts to Martello towers, from the ambitious Royal Military Canal to wartime airfields and underground Cold War installations.

978 0 7509 4460 9

Folklore of Kent

FRAN & GEOFF DOEL

Kent boasts a plethora of characterising traditions, including hop-growing, smuggling and saints. All this reflects the curious history and geography of the area. Bounded by the sea on three sides, Kent has a rich maritime heritage of trade, invasions and sea-lore. Also covered are seasonal harvet traditions, witchcraft, saints and holy wells. The background and songs surrounding fruit and hop-growing is also explained. This book charts the traditional culture of a populous and culturally significant southern county.

978 0 7524 2628 0

sit our website and discover thousands of other History Press books.

·w.thehistorypress.co.uk